About the Author

Steven Saunders trained as a chef at London's Savoy Hotel. He went on to manage for a group of East Anglian hotels, then at the age of 25 he and his wife Sally bought the Pink Geranium, a restaurant in a thatched cottage in the village of Melbourn, near Cambridge. Nine years later, the restaurant's many accolades include an Association for Catering Excellence Award for Restaurant of the Year 1995, a Michelin Red 'M', two AA rosettes, an Ackerman Four Leaf Clover, the Egon Ronay Arrow and high praise in *The Good Food Guide*. Steven was voted Young Restaurateur of the Year in 1991, and in 1995 the Pink Geranium was voted one of the top twenty most popular restaurants in Britain. Besides being chef/proprietor, Steven also runs a cookery school, a catering company and a delicatessen service from the restaurant.

Steven Saunders is also known to millions as one of the stars of BBC2's top-rating cookery game show, *Ready Steady Cook*, produced by Bazal Productions. He has also been resident chef on *Good Morning with Anne and Nick* and *Fully Booked*, and has hosted his own radio shows for nine years besides many other media appearances. His magazine column, 'A Fresh Look', in which he advised the trade on the best fresh produce available, ran for three years in *The Caterer and Hotelkeeper*; he has gone on to consult for several national supermarket chains and food companies.

Steven has often contributed to *BBC Good Food* as well as local and national newspapers. When his original restaurant was destroyed by thatch fire, he reopened in his own living room, and wrote his first book, *Only the Best*, which was published in 1993.

Steven and Sally Saunders have two daughters, Serena and Stefanie.

CHEF'S SECRETS

STEVEN SAUNDERS

 # CHEF'S
SECRETS
Mastering the
Art of Good Food

BⓈXTREE

First published in Great Britain in 1996 by
Boxtree Limited, Broadwall House, 21 Broadwall, London SE1 9PL

1 3 5 7 9 10 8 6 4 2

ISBN 0 7522 0581 1

Text design and layouts by Roger Daniels
Cover design by Slatter-Anderson
Photography by Philip Wilkins

Printed and bound in Great Britain

A CIP catalogue entry for this book is available from the British Library

Acknowledgements

Working on a book like this is not an entirely solitary experience. Thanks go to a number of people who helped in its production: my agent Michael Ladkin, Gordon Scott Wise, Senior Editor at Boxtree, Graham Hart who produced the first draft, copy editor Deborah Savage, Sue Nicholas who transcribed my tapes, Philip Wilkins for his stunning photography, and Bridget and all those who assisted him. Thanks also go to Jim Stanton at Slatter-Anderson for his great cover design, Roger Daniels for his book design, Peter Rowe at Lay and Wheeler Wines, Colchester, for selecting the wines accompanying the recipes, Hyams and Cockerton Ltd for supplying the fruits and vegetables photographed in the book, all the staff at the Pink Geranium (in particular Paul Murfitt and the other chefs who provided valuable advice), and, as ever, Sally who had her kitchen turned into a photographic studio for an entire week for this book. Thanks to you all.

STEVEN SAUNDERS

Contents

Introduction

There were occasions during the writing of this book when I was able to stand away from the task and ask myself exactly what I wanted to achieve. I usually came back to three basic points.

Firstly, I wanted to share my enthusiasm and knowledge with others. This is the reason I run so many

cookery schools, and why I enjoy appearing on television and writing in magazines. I do genuinely love cooking, the food, the people and the pleasure it gives. In particular, I enjoy sharing some of the tricks and techniques that I have learned and then watching the delight on people's faces as recipes work out perfectly and apparent problems are solved.

Secondly, I wanted to share my approach to cooking with others. All chefs have their special strengths and preferences. I hope you will gain an insight into mine through following these recipes. Importantly, also, through using my secrets, I hope that you will find that my style is within your reach. The exotic-sounding recipes and complex presentations and that we prepare at the Pink Geranium are, if not always simple, easily within reach of a keen amateur cook.

Thirdly, I wanted to encourage creativity in cooking. For every ten recipes within this book there are probably a hundred variations. These are waiting for you to invent and perfect. Once you feel confident, you can try substituting various ingredients or 'mixing and matching' main courses with different accompaniments. Try some of my ideas for alternative sauces or attempt variations of my constructions. All through the writing of the book, my recipes were undergoing change; there are, in fact, very few classic recipes that are exactly the same time after time. It is up to you to experiment.

Most of the dishes I've included should take little more than half an hour to assemble, except for those involving braising or a confit. The secret is to prepare as much as you possibly can in advance (we call this *mise en place*), allowing you to spend more time with your guests and a minimal amount of time in the kitchen. Delia Smith once described herself as being on rung one of the ladder of culinary expertise; perhaps this book represents rung two. But I hope that my tips and notes will help you overcome any worry barriers, and that you will move from being good cooks to excellent cooks, and from good hosts to superb culinary entertainers.

STEVEN SAUNDERS

Using this book

Before you set about using the recipes, there are a few general points to note.

Quantities
Each individual recipe will work with the amounts shown. However, you might be well advised to have more than the minimum for some of the basics like oil, seasoning, wine, stock and so on. As you will know, different room temperatures, different ovens or maybe just something to do with the way a particular person likes to work can all cause minor differences in the way a recipe works out. So, be prepared to chop and change a little until you have the result that suits you.

Seasoning
I always season savoury dishes with salt and, usually, a pinch of freshly ground white pepper. Black pepper is more of a spice and should not be used as a seasoning: it is often too overpowering. The salt I use is standard table salt but I sometimes use coarse sea salt for extra flavour and texture; but remember, it is stronger than table salt.

Olive oil and cooking oils

Remember that olive oil tastes of olives and, unless you want that Mediterranean flavour penetrating a dish, you should avoid frying or cooking with it. I use grapeseed oil and, sometimes, clarified butter for frying, unless I want other flavours involved. My advice is to keep your frying oil simple and use the best extra virgin olive oil for salad dressings and oily sauces like the Vierge Sauce and Antiboise Sauce recipes in this book.

Another tip is to avoid buying expensive herbal oils because you can always infuse your own choice of herbs in good olive oil for the same results and for, probably, half the price.

Garlic

I use garlic a lot in recipes: where would we be without it? However, if it is overdone it will spoil other flavours with its bitter strength, so keep the quantities of garlic to those given. Always use fresh garlic; garlic from bottles, cans and tubes is not comparable. There is little taste difference between red and white fresh garlic, so use the one you are most familiar with unless otherwise specified.

Some recipes call for garlic to be crushed to a paste. You can use a garlic crusher for this, but they are fiddly to clean and not really necessary. To crush garlic without a crusher, finely chop it first and then sprinkle it with a little salt. Use the flat of a knife blade (the heavier the better) to reduce it to a paste; the salt crystals help to crush the flesh. Or use a pestle and mortar.

Presentation

It's funny how the presentation of food changes over the years, just like clothes fashions do. I can remember several food fashions since my training in the 1970s; the '90s are very different. Food is now presented more unadulterated, often using the flavours and spices of other countries (especially the Mediterranean and Far East); we call this fusion cuisine.

At the Pink Geranium we are a young team, who live and breathe the kitchen, and new ideas are always in the air. The presentation in this book is what would be called 'fashionable' at time of writing, but I also believe it is simple, neat and tidy. Each recipe uses a variety of flavours and techniques, but I don't think any are over-complicated. The physical assembly described and shown in the colour photographs tends towards the tall, elegant and rather round – something of my trademark style, but essentially quick ways to make a delicious dish stunning too.

WINE Next to each main dish I have included a wine suggestion which I believe works well with its flavours. None of these should be too hard to find (or too expensive!); if you don't find them in the wine section of your supermarket, talk to your local wine merchant about what he or she recommends from their selection, and the best vintages available. We also run a wine club at the Pink Geranium! I am indebted to Peter Rowe from Lay and Wheeler Wines in Colchester (01206 764446) for his help in making these selections.

Metric measurements

I tend to use a mixture of metric and imperial measurements when I am cooking: I use good, old-fashioned guesswork too. Today, we do all our purchasing in metric amounts, so I have converted the recipes in this book to metric. But if you feel uncomfortable with this, here are some simple conversion tables to help you. These are based upon the recommendations of the Good Housekeeping Institute.
I have also included spoon measurements in ml quantities.

Liquid measurements		
30ml	1fl oz	
60ml	2fl oz	
150ml	5fl oz	¼ pint
300ml	10fl oz	½ pint
450ml	15fl oz	¾ pint
600ml	20fl oz	1 pint
900ml	30fl oz	1½ pints
1 litre	34fl oz	1¾ pints

Solid measurements	
25g	1oz
50g	2oz
100g	4oz
225g	8oz
350g	12oz
450g	1lb
1kg	2.2lb

Spoon measurements	
1 teaspoon	5ml spoon
1 dessertspoon	10ml spoon
1 tablespoon	15ml spoon

On BBC2's *Ready Steady Cook* (see Twenty-minute Marvels, page 79) the competing chefs are given a basic larder to use in conjunction with the five ingredients given to us by an audience member. Here follows – not in any order of priority –

a list of ingredients which I recommend adding to your own basics. I always try to keep some of the following on hand, and they will help you considerably as you begin to master the art of good food.

Dried Spices
mustard (seeds)
paprika (ground)
cayenne pepper (ground)
turmeric
    (whole or ground)
nutmeg
    (whole or ground)
cumin (ground)
cardamom (pods)
cinnamon (stick or bark)
star anise (whole)
cloves (whole)
dried chillies (whole)
black pepper
    (whole corns to grind)
migonette pepper (crushed
    corns)
white pepper (ground)
sea salt
    (coarse crystals)
mixed spice (ground)
pure saffron
coriander (ground)
caraway seeds (whole)
sesame seeds (whole)

Dried Herbs
tarragon
bay leaves
herbes de Provence
oregano

Fresh herbs
basil (green or purple)
coriander
chives
parsley (flat leaf)
mint
rosemary
wild thyme
horseradish
    (freshly grated)
ginger (fresh root)
shallots
garlic
vanilla (fresh pods)
lemon grass

Bottled Sauces/Oils
truffle essence
    or truffle oil
soy sauce
honey
balsamic vinegar
sherry vinegar
wholegrain mustard
tomato purée
grapeseed (cooking oil)
extra virgin olive oil
    (for salad dressings and
    sauces)
capers in vinegar
black olives in brine

Fresh Fruit
limes
lemons
oranges
Italian plum tomatoes

Other
Free range eggs
    (Italian, if available, for
    pasta making)
muslin
    (for passing sauces
    through)
baking parchment
    (or greaseproof paper)
tin foil
Puy lentils
dried haricot beans
wild rice
risotto rice
potato flour
leaf gelatine
baking powder
pasta flour
    (00 strength)
fresh yeast
wine (cheap, to cook with)
polenta flour

For further information about these ingredients and to order anything you can't find locally, contact:

V Benoist Limited
8-10 Eldon Way
London NW10 7QX
Tel 0181 965 9531

The Pink Geranium also has a delicatessen service. Write to us at:

The Pink Geranium
Melbourn, Royston
Herts. SG8 6DX
Tel 01763 260215
or 01763 262503
Fax 01763 262110

Canapés and First Courses

Canapés are not something that you will always want to serve when entertaining because they can be time-consuming and fiddly to prepare. Your efforts will mostly be geared towards the first course, main course and pudding.

However, canapés can repay the effort of preparation. They are ideal for people to nibble with the first drink, while you are cooking, and are often a talking point that helps guests to relax. More than that, canapés are perfect for finger buffets and drinks parties, at Christmas, for example. They are easy to eat when you are standing up, so are ideal for informal parties.

I have put the canapé dishes first, followed by suggestions for first courses. First courses are always a very important part of a meal and you can afford to be very creative with them. Most of the first courses recommended here take a little time but they all look excellent on the plate and will bring admiring comments from guests.

First-course ideas can be developed into light lunches or main courses. Often, a slight increase in quantities or the addition of a few vegetables or a bread will effect this transformation. The chapter on main courses will give you plenty of ideas of what vegetables go well with fish, meat and so on. As in all cooking, the key is to think creatively around the basic idea.

Canapé Croûtes

It doesn't matter what type of bread you use for these; it's usually the topping that takes the attention. I normally use simple white sliced bread, with the crusts removed. The key is to pour the oil into the centre of the baking tray and touch both sides of your small pieces of bread in it. Make sure both sides are coated, but don't drench them. Repeat and repeat until all croûtes are coated.

If you are using your own bread, you can add extra flavours to the dough which will make them even more interesting, but more time-consuming.

white, brown or wholemeal bread or brioche
olive oil
salt and pepper

1 Preheat the oven to 180°C/350°F/Gas Mark 4. Cut the bread into small circles, 2–3cm in diameter, with a small pastry cutter.
2 Put them on a baking tray, dip both sides in the olive oil and season liberally.
3 Bake until dry, crisp and slightly brown. Take them away from the heat immediately and leave to cool before serving.

Notes on toppings

• One of the simplest and most successful combinations is to spread Tapenade (page 9) on the croûtes. Serve with a sprig of chervil.

• Variations of salmon also work very well with croûtes. Rillette of Salmon (page 25), Smoked Salmon Roulade (page 21) and Ceviche of Salmon (page 24) are all ideal – and all described in this chapter. For salmon toppings, you may wish to make the croûtes slightly larger.

• Like many canapés, croûtes offer an ideal opportunity to experiment. Light, soft cheeses with herbs are perfect. Just ensure that your choice is delicately flavoured and that the texture blends well with the crunchiness of the croûtes.

WINE Champagne or sparkling wines go well with most canapés, and get the proceedings off to a bubbly start.

Tapenade

This has a wonderful and original flavour. It is very Mediterranean and evokes warm, summer days. As you will see elsewhere in the book, it is very useful for adding to other recipes, both canapés and first and main courses. Fish benefit greatly from tapenade.

Tapenade keeps well and is a great stop-gap. Use it on toasted French bread, with a few tomatoes, for a delicious lunchtime snack.

With tapenade, I should also say that it is an easy item to keep in the fridge, too. This increases its appeal. I sometimes finish up my day with a little tapenade and cheese or crisp salad, eaten with crackers and a glass of red wine. Delicious.

ENOUGH FOR ABOUT 30 CROUTES

250g black olives, stoned
50g canned, salted anchovies, drained
25g capers
1 garlic clove
juice of 1 lemon or lime
1 tablespoon olive oil
salt and pepper (optional)
large bunch of parsley (optional)

1 Put all the ingredients in the food processor and blend them for a few minutes. Remove the processor's top and blend manually for a couple of minutes.
2 Taste and, if necessary, add seasoning and re-blend until it starts to form a paste.

Notes

• Tapenade will keep in an airtight container in the refrigerator for at least a month.
• Here is another ideal opportunity to experiment, altering quantities and, most importantly, flavours. Try, for example, adding 2-3 skinned and seeded tomatoes.

WINE Champagne or sparkling wines go well with most canapés, and get the proceedings off to a bubbly start.

Baked Goat's Cheese
with tapenade crust and 'sun-dried' peppers

The method of this recipe is the key; the ingredients can differ. You don't have to use a tapenade crust; try herb breadcrumbs (page 168). Similarly, the type of cheese and leaf can vary. Baked peppers (page 63) can replace the 'sun-dried' peppers (dried in a very low oven but with a similar effect). I suggest lollo rosso, radicchio, rocket and curly endive as a good mixture of leaves, and a cylindrical English goat's cheese. A good relationship with your grocer is helpful. I have always been impressed with the service received from staff working on the delicatessen counters of large supermarkets, too. Try asking for help.

50g Tapenade (page 9)
100g breadcrumbs
1 egg
25ml milk (goat's milk, if possible)
mixed salad leaves
250ml Antiboise Sauce (page 104)
4 small goat's cheeses
100g plain flour, seasoned

For the sun-dried peppers:
2 red peppers
1kg coarse sea salt
4 garlic cloves
leaves of a large fresh thyme sprig, chopped
100ml olive oil

1 Mix the tapenade with the fresh breadcrumbs and taste the mixture. Season, if necessary.
2 Mix the egg with a little milk, to produce an egg wash. Simply dip the cheeses into the flour and then into the egg, until covered completely. Roll them in the tapenade crumbs, until fully coated. Set aside.

3 Preheat the oven to 140°C/250°F/Gas Mark 1. Cut the peppers into small, thin slices and remove any pith and seeds.
4 Smother a baking tray with sea salt and lay the peppers on top.
5 Sprinkle them with the chopped garlic and thyme.
6 Leave overnight or for about 8 hours in the very low oven, until they are shrunken and nearly completely dry.
7 Carefully brush off the garlic and salt and reserve the peppers in a little olive oil (just enough to coat the strips). Refrigerate until needed.
8 Preheat the oven to 180°C/350°F/Gas Mark 4. Warm a small frying-pan with a little oil and seal the goat's cheese on all sides, being careful not to burn the breadcrumbs.
9 Put the cheese in the oven for 4-5 minutes, until soft.
10 Serve the cheese with the warmed peppers, using Antiboise Sauce (page 104) to dress the leaves.

WINE Any Sauvignon Blanc is excellent with goat's cheese; Sancerre is particularly well-known for its affinity.

Notes
• You could deep-fry the cheese, but take care not to burn it: golden brown is what we are after.
• I often serve the cheese in the centre of a Circle Salad (see photo), which adds colour. The antiboise mentioned is probably my favourite (and very simple) but you could have a simple vinaigrette sauce, or a balsamic vinegar dressing.

Bruschetta

The first time I had bruschetta was at the Savoy Hotel in London, about 15 years ago. I just thought it was simple French bread with a little something on top. Biting into it, however, I realised that the bread had been soaked in garlic oil – and I loved it.

Since then, bruschetta has often been a life-saver when I'm pushed for time or need to delay serving a meal. It is a tasty, easy to prepare canapé, ideal when you want something to serve with drinks. It can be quite filling, however, so beware. It also makes a particularly good finger food for cocktail and drinks parties.

SERVES 12

1 small fresh baguette
3 garlic cloves, crushed
olive oil
4-5 small Italian plum tomatoes, sliced
fresh basil sprigs
100g mozzarella cheese, sliced
salt and pepper

1 Preheat the oven to 180°C/350°F/Gas Mark 4. Cut the bread into lozenge shapes, about 2cm thick.
2 Peel and crush the garlic cloves and sprinkle them over the bread. Coat the bread with olive oil, put the slices on a baking tray and bake until they are crisp.
3 Remove the bread and put slices of tomato and a basil sprig on each bread slice. Season only at this point.
4 Top with mozzarella and lightly grill or bake until the cheese has melted. Serve warm.

Notes

• In choosing toppings, you can think along the same lines as croûtes, remembering to balance your choice of topping with the crunchy and crisp nature of the bruschetta. Keeping bruschetta crisp is important.
• Try melted goat's cheese with Tapenade (page 9) or marinated tomatoes (using balsamic vinegar and a little sugar to get superb tastes).
• Make small bruschetta for canapés, slightly larger ones for a finger buffet. My choice is to wait for a summer lunch. Try bruschetta, salad and a chilled Chardonnay and your visitors will be very impressed.

Gruyère *Beignets*

These deep-fried 'puffs' are ideal for a finger buffet or as a small canapé. You just alter the size to suit your requirements.

I have included this recipe because it is very simple. I used to think that *beignets* were time-consuming because of the need to make a batter mixture; this recipe avoids that complication. It was one of my chefs who introduced me to the idea of whisking the egg whites; this works perfectly, so do try it.

SERVES 8

7 egg whites
squeeze of lemon juice
250g Gruyère cheese, grated
pinch of ground mixed spice
bunch of fresh coriander, finely chopped
fresh tarragon sprig, finely chopped
fresh breadcrumbs
oil for deep-frying
salt and pepper

1 Whisk the egg whites to peaks, with a little lemon juice to help stiffen them. Add the cheese.

2 Add the spices and herbs to the cheese mixture and season to taste.

3 The mixture should be fairly stiff; if necessary, add more cheese. Roll little balls or quenelles (3-5cm) of the mixture in the breadcrumbs (see method for quenelles, page 170). Heat the oil and deep-fry at about 170°C until golden brown. Serve warm.

Notes

• This is the kind of recipe where you can experiment with available herbs and cheeses, to see what suits your taste.

• Please also note that the temperature of 170°C is important. This is the perfect heat for deep-frying vegetables, and *beignets*. Deep-frying doesn't necessitate the use of a deep-fat pan or, even, deep fat! You can use oil about 5cm deep for frying, turning the contents regularly, but be sure you take the pan off the heat afterwards, as this can be a fire hazard.

Gâteaux of Home-smoked Chicken and Avocado
with citrus dressing

The first thing to say about this dish is how easy it is to smoke your own meat or fish – but it is smelly! I am not saying it isn't a messy process (there's no denying that the kitchen does fill with smoke!) but it is certainly easier than you might think. For the home cook, there is great satisfaction in doing your own smoking. Even more importantly, perhaps, the meat or fish will retain their moisture and texture much better with home smoking. The wood chippings you use are up to you, but oak or beech are tried and tested. I often use the wood from my gas barbecue for smoky results, too.

In other respects, this dish resembles the style of the rillette and crab gâteau starters. The gâteau will be circular in shape, a delight in itself and enhanced by your choice of sauce or dressing. It provides an excellent opportunity for you to experiment with presentation.

I also feel that this recipe gives you an insight into my thinking about tackling cheaper and less exotic ingredients, such as chicken. Yes, chicken can be bland but, with a little thought and creativity, almost anything can be made exotic and exciting. Money is always a consideration and chicken is an inexpensive ingredient, which is particularly important if you have more expensive items to buy for the main course.

SERVES 6

250g chicken breast, smoked (see opposite) and finely chopped
1 ripe avocado, finely sliced
juice of 1 lemon
pinch of salt
150g fromage frais or natural yoghurt

For the citrus dressing:
50g icing sugar
juice of 1 lemon, 1 lime, 1 orange and 1 pink grapefruit
100ml olive oil
fresh chives, finely chopped
6 fresh chervil sprigs
salt and pepper

To smoke the chicken (see photos):
1 Pour about 5cm of beech or oak shavings into a heavy-based pan, cover with a conical strainer and top with a lid. Leave the pan on a high heat until the smoke has built up.

2 Slice the chicken breast in half lengthways, brush it with a little oil and sear it on the strainer, with the lid on, for a minute on each side.

 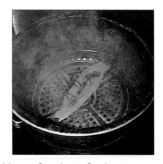

3 Reduce the heat slightly, and leave for about 6 minutes, until the chicken has cooked through. Remove from the heat and leave to rest (do not overcook or it will be tough).

For the gâteaux:
1 Mix together the chicken, avocado, lemon juice and salt. Fold in two-thirds of the fromage frais or yoghurt and mould the mixture in six oiled 6cm straight-sided metal pastry rings, set on serving plates. Do not fill the moulds quite to the top – leave about 1cm unfilled.
2 Spread over the remaining fromage frais or yoghurt and level with a palette knife. Remove each ring carefully, so that the gâteaux stand in neat, round shapes.
3 Make the dressing by whisking the icing sugar, fruit juices and olive oil in a glass bowl until thoroughly blended. Sprinkle the chives over this mixture. Season and taste.
4 Spoon a little of the citrus dressing around each chicken gâteau. Garnish with chervil sprigs, and a little Tomato Concassé (page 25).

WINE Look for an Australian Chardonnay with a peachy hint (most mid-priced Australian Chardonnays have this quality).

Notes
• The dressing I have recommended is citrus based, with the sharpness softened slightly by the sugar. On this citrus theme, I have served the gâteaux with Pickled Cucumber (page 138), with considerable success.

Chicken-liver *Parfait*

A *parfait* is a silky-smooth paté-style dish, rich and full of flavour. If you like the flavours of chicken livers, this is the recipe for you. It really does repay the effort. The recipe is very time-consuming to tackle just for canapés but you could use the trimmings of the *parfait* (left over from making it as a starter). I can't speak too highly of this particular dish; it has been a great success for the Pink Geranium. None of it should be wasted!

I have suggested serving the *parfait* on croûtes for a canapé. For a first course, serve a slice on toasted brioche, with a Circle Salad (page 178) around it.

SERVES 6 AS A STARTER OR MORE AS CANAPES

25ml cooking oil
6 shallots, finely chopped
4 garlic cloves, finely chopped
150ml Madeira
150ml port
150ml cognac
250g chicken livers
10 egg yolks
250ml double cream
pinch of ground allspice
salt and pepper

To serve:
Canapé Croûtes (page 8), or Brioche (page 142), toasted

1 Preheat the oven to 150°C/300°F/Gas Mark 2. Sweat the shallots and garlic in the oil in a saucepan. Add the Madeira, port and cognac; reduce by half. Leave to cool completely and pass through a sieve into a clean bowl.

2 Cut away the galls of the chicken livers and purée the livers in a food processor, with the shallot mixture. Make sure the mixture is cold before processing.

3 Add the egg yolks and cream and taste the raw mixture (yuk! If you really can't face this idea, put a little of the livers in a pan, warm and taste). Adjust the seasoning, with salt, pepper and allspice.

4 Pass the livers through a fine sieve into a clean bowl.

5 Pour this mixture into a terrine mould lined with cling film or foil and bake in a bain-marie for about 1 hour and 20 minutes.

6 Leave to cool at room temperature for up to 2 hours and then let it rest in the fridge, preferably for a day, before slicing and serving.

Notes

• One difficulty is knowing how long to cook this dish. I have suggested about 1 hour and 20 minutes but this really depends upon the size of the terrine and so on. The first way to check is to pour the water away, and gently shake the dish. It should be wobbly in the centre, but not on the sides. The liver mixture should be served slightly pink, so it's important not to over-cook it. If the outsides are relatively solid, and the inside wobbles, it is done. The natural setting process will firm up the dish for you. (If it is not wobbly, the outside will be overdone.) If you are not sure, insert a trussing needle in the centre and withdraw it. The needle should be hot and dry.

• I recommend non-PVC cling film as I use it a lot in my kitchen. Some people are less happy about its use; baking parchment, or tin foil, are also suitable.

Smoked Breast of Wood Pigeon
with onion marmalade and cassis *jus*

Here is a dish that takes time to prepare and is fiddly, but the result will be a marvellous example of your culinary skills for a special meal.

This is also a good, warming, winter recipe. I can imagine it on a cold lunch time, followed by a short walk. I have suggested wood pigeon but squab pigeon, a farmed variety, may be better. Not much game is as good, or better, farmed, but squab is an exception. Squab may be more expensive but the birds will be very juicy and tender, having been fed on good corn. Wild wood pigeon varies in quality; it can sometimes be a little tough, but it is a lot cheaper.

The onion marmalade complements the smokiness of the wood pigeon. A further contrast in flavour and texture can be made by putting small amounts of marmalade in a pastry tartlet (page 144) and serving the wood pigeon on top. Your decision, perhaps, will be based on the appetites of the people you are cooking for and the time you have available.

The essence here is *mise en place*, that is, 'putting into place', or preparing in advance. The pigeon can be smoked, the marmalade made, the tartlets cooked: all you have to do is heat, combine and construct at the last minute.

Home-smoking (page 15) creates lovely flavours but I strongly recommend you do it well away from the time of serving; smoking is a messy business. Take my word for it: you can't buy smoked pigeon as tasty as the home-smoked kind, and this way you get it perfectly cooked.

SERVES 4

4 pigeon breasts, smoked (page 15)

For the marmalade:
2 onions, thinly sliced
100ml oil
50ml white wine vinegar
100ml dry white wine
50g caster sugar
pinch of salt

For the sauce:
120ml Veal *Jus* (page 100)
50ml *crème de cassis* liqueur

1 Smoke the pigeon breasts off the carcass (see page 15) for 2-3 minutes on each side.
2 Put the veal *jus* on the stove and allow it to reduce. Preheat the oven to 230°C/450°F/Gas Mark 8.
3 Make the marmalade by sweating the sliced onions in a saucepan in the oil, until tender. Add the vinegar, white wine and sugar. Stir well and allow the onions to absorb the liquor. When all of the liquor is absorbed, the onions should appear translucent and caramelized and taste sweet and sour. Season with a little salt.
4 To finish the pigeon breasts, simply heat an ovenproof frying-pan until it's very hot and sear the breasts both sides. Put the pan in the oven for about 3 minutes.
5 Remove and allow the breasts to rest for 3-4 minutes. Slice them in half, horizontally, and serve them neatly on the marmalade (ideally, in a pastry tartlet case).
6 When the *jus* has reduced to become quite thick, add a splash of *cassis*, taste, season and taste again. Bring the sauce back to the boil and serve it around the pigeon breasts.

A spicy Rhône red such as Gigondas.

Notes
- For extra flavour, poach apple slices in the marmalade.

Honey-roasted Boneless Quail
with cabbage, garlic and lime cream and deep-fried basil leaves

Although I generally suggest cooking game on the bone, for flavour, I recommend, for this recipe, using boneless quail. Not only is it very fiddly to remove the small bones from quail when eating them, but it is also much harder to stuff a bird with bones. The stuffing is vital; it is this that provides the variety of tastes that will make this dish one of your future favourites.

Also note that the sauce doesn't use game stock, so it's very simple and light in taste. Overall, the dish is complex in terms of the marriage of flavours. It is fundamentally citric but will not seem sharp.

Don't be put off by the length of the ingredients and method; it is relatively easy, and a recipe that our customers at the Pink Geranium have enthused over for a long time.

SERVES 4

4 boneless quail
1 Savoy cabbage
25g butter or 2 tablespoons oil
freshly grated nutmeg
salt
20 fresh basil leaves
oil, for deep-frying
Tomato *Concassé* (page 25), to garnish

For the stuffing:
grated zest and juice of 3 limes and 1 lemon
1 garlic clove, crushed to a paste
1 tablespoon chopped fresh coriander
about 50g breadcrumbs (preferably brioche)
25g unsalted butter, melted
salt and pepper

For the sauce:
2 garlic cloves, crushed to a paste
3 shallots, finely chopped
25g butter or 2 tablespoons oil
juice of 3 limes
250ml double cream
salt and pepper

For the stuffing:
1 Add the lime and lemon zest and juice and garlic, herbs and seasoning to the breadcrumbs.
2 Pour the butter on to the breadcrumbs to bind the mixture and mix well.

For the sauce:
1 Put the garlic and shallots in a deep, thick-bottomed saucepan and sweat them in the butter or oil.
2 Add the lime juice and reduce this mixture to a glaze (a bit like the reduction for *Beurre Blanc*, page 110).
3 Pour in the double cream and reduce again until thick and creamy; this should take about 10 minutes.
4 Pour into a clean container and allow to cool. The sauce can be seasoned when you re-heat it, or serve it immediately if preferred (see Notes).

For the cabbage:
1 Remove the outer leaves, discard any damaged ones and cut out the stalky bits with a sharp knife.
2 Roll the leaves together and shred them finely (this is called a *chiffonade*).
3 Fry the leaves in a saucepan in a little melted butter until soft and tender; season with salt and a little nutmeg. Taste before serving.

5 Roast on a metal baking tray for about 15 minutes until golden brown and firm to the touch.

6 Allow to rest out of the oven for a couple of minutes before serving.

7 In a deep-fryer or in a frying-pan with hot oil, drop the basil leaves into the fat, carefully avoiding the spitting that the water in the leaves will cause. Remove and drain on kitchen paper; season with salt.

To serve:

1 On a large plate, arrange the cabbage in the middle in a little pile, using a ring.

2 Put the quail on top and pour the sauce around (but you don't need very much sauce).

3 Scatter the deep-fried basil leaves around, with a sprinkling of Tomato *Concassé*, to add colour. Serve immediately.

WINE A supple floral Pinot Noir-based rosé like Sancerre Rosé, or a top-class rosé Champagne such as Laurent Perrier or Krug Rosé.

For the quail:

1 Preheat the oven to 230°C/450°F/Gas Mark 8. Open out each quail and remove any little bones remaining, such as wing bones.

2 Fill the centre of each quail with the stuffing.

3 Fold the quail together to form its original boneless shape.

4 Baste each quail with a little melted butter and season.

Notes

• You can use any soft green herb you prefer instead of the basil. The deep-frying does not require a lot of oil (see Deep Fried Herbs, page 169), so the herb can also be shallow-fried.

• The sauce benefits by being allowed to stand and cool down, which brings out the flavours even more. It will keep in a fridge for 2-3 days, but is best served within 24 hours.

Salad of Oriental Gravad Lax
with lime and coriander dressing

The words *gravad lax* refer to the way the salmon is marinated. The oriental nature of the dish comes out in the use of ginger, shallots, lemon grass and coriander in the dressing. I think this is a superb starter and it also works as a major element on a buffet table.

In simple terms, there are three parts to the recipe. First you prepare a paste to dress the salmon before you marinate it. You then leave it to marinate for at least 24 hours (48 hours is better). Finally, you serve with the lime and coriander dressing. The dressing is light in flavour and should be served sparingly. The icing sugar is the key; the sweetness of the sugar detracts from any sharpness created by the citrus juices.

One other point to remember before you start: the paste used with the salmon in the marinade is easy to make and its appearance is unimportant as you don't actually serve it.

SERVES 4

1 side of fresh farmed salmon, about 2kg
150ml jar of Dijon mustard
125g caster sugar
125g sea salt
50ml cooking brandy
50ml white wine
250ml virgin olive oil
juice of 4 oranges
large bunch of fresh coriander

For the paste:
large bunch of fresh coriander
3 stalks of lemon grass, finely chopped, or ground lemon grass
1.5cm piece of fresh ginger, peeled
grated zest of 4 oranges
grated zest and juice of 2 limes
3 shallots
4 garlic cloves

For the lime and coriander dressing:
25g icing sugar
juice of 6 limes and 1 lemon
100ml virgin or extra-virgin olive oil
pinch of salt
finely chopped fresh coriander

1 Spread one side of the salmon with the mustard.
2 In a food processor, blend the paste ingredients to a fairly smooth consistency. Add a little olive oil, if necessary.
3 Spread this paste over the mustard side of the salmon and sprinkle a mixture of equal amounts of sugar and salt over the paste and over the other side of the salmon.
4 Mix the brandy, wine and olive oil with the orange juice. Put the salmon into this marinade (in a deep dish), cover with cling film and allow to cure in a refrigerator for 24-48 hours.
5 After 48 hours wash the paste off in cold water. Finely chop the remaining bunch of coriander. Cover one side of the salmon with the coriander and slice it thinly to serve.
6 Dress the salmon with the lime and coriander dressing (see opposite) and serve.

For the lime and coriander dressing

1 In a bowl, mix the icing sugar and lime and lemon juice together, until the sugar has dissolved.

2 Gradually pour on the olive oil.

3 Season with salt and coriander and taste. Adjust the seasoning, if necessary, and serve.

WINE Australian or New Zealand Riesling.

Notes

• I recommend placing the salmon around a neat Central Salad (page 178). Any mustard can be used instead of Dijon; Meaux wholegrain mustard is excellent.

Smoked Salmon Roulade

This came from one of the chefs at the Pink Geranium who wanted to introduce a slightly more adventurous (and expensive!) element to our canapés. We played around with several ideas before settling for an adaptation of a recipe we were using as a first course. Thus, with double the quantities shown here, you could make this into a terrific first course.

To reduce the cost, use smoked trout instead of salmon.

SERVES ABOUT 10 AS A CANAPE

1 quarter-side (about 8 large slices) of smoked salmon
8 large spinach leaves
125g Rillette of Salmon mixture (page 25)
salt and pepper

1 Put the sliced smoked salmon on a large rectangle of cling film (about 30 × 50 cm), forming a flat, smaller, rectangle of fish.

2 Clean the spinach thoroughly and then blanch it in boiling, salted water for 30 seconds. Put the leaves into iced (or very cold) water to refresh them quickly. Squeeze the leaves to eliminate the water and spread them over the smoked salmon rectangle. Season the leaves lightly.

3 Spread the salmon rillette mixture evenly and thinly over the leaves.

4 Carefully roll up the roulade in the cling film, to form a neat, tight, circular roulade. Make sure the cling film doesn't get rolled into the roulade. Twist the cling film ends like a Christmas cracker, to secure them. Put the roulade on a tray in the freezer.

5 When you want to use the roulade, take it out of the freezer, unwrap it and leave it for a few minutes in the kitchen; then slice it into small, thin discs. You will not be able to cut it thinly unless it is partly frozen.

Notes

• A touch of olive oil on a pastry brush, spread gently over the cut roulade discs just before serving, gives them added sheen. I recommend placing these on Canapé Croûtes (page 8).

• The roulade needs to be partly frozen before cutting but, once sliced, it will thaw out quickly.

Tapenade-fried Crisp Red Mullet

with _vierge_ sauce and roasted tomatoes

Mediterranean flavours really came into their own in the early 1990s. I think it was partly a result of the wonderful vegetable varieties that became available and partly because of the interest in the 'Mediterranean diet': foods cooked with olive oil, garlic, citrus fruits and so on. In this dish, the Vierge Sauce is another Mediterranean influence and, of course, the mullet itself is a Mediterranean fish.

This is a light starter that has always been popular with diners who have chosen a heavier, meat main course. The flavours are excellent, and the presentation is superb.

I mention pin-boning: this simply means using tweezers or other fine implements to remove from the mullet all the very fine bones that may be left after the filleting.

For the roasted tomatoes and caramelized onions:
light olive oil
1 onion, thinly sliced
pinch of caster sugar
pinch of salt
4 plum tomatoes, quartered
25ml dry white wine
salt and pepper

For the mullet:
2 medium red mullet, filleted and pin-boned
150g plain flour, seasoned
about 50g Tapenade (page 9)
light olive oil
salt and pepper

To serve:
75ml Vierge Sauce (page 111)

For the roasted tomatoes and onions
1 Preheat the oven to 230°C/450°F/Gas Mark 8. Add a little oil to a very hot ovenproof frying-pan, allow it to smoke a little and add the onion. Sprinkle with a little caster sugar and salt and allow to caramelize slightly, and cook until tender.
2 Sear the tomatoes in a very hot frying pan until browned on the skin side. Use a pan with an ovenproof handle. De-glaze (a process whereby a spirit or wine is added to a hot pan to bring together all of the flavours, including those from the bottom of the pan) by adding a little white wine to the juices and stirring. Roast the tomatoes in the oven for 5 minutes, until soft. Season, remove and reserve.

For the mullet
1 Coat the fillets with the seasoned flour and shake and pat them well, to remove excess flour.
2 Spread the tapenade on the flesh side of the fish.
Heat the oil in a frying-pan until it's smoking and fry the fish, skin-side down. Press gently on the fillets, to prevent them from curling up.
3 Turn the fish over and seal the tapenade side. Cook for 2-3 minutes. Leave in the pan but remove the pan from the heat and leave them to rest briefly.
4 Serve the fish skin-side up (for presentation purposes) on a small bed of the tomatoes and onions, packed inside a ring, with a little Vierge Sauce around (see photo).

 A really top-flight Soave or Lugana.

Notes
• Mullet is a fish that should be served quickly after cooking, so ensure that everything else is ready before you begin the final cooking.
• When cooking the tomatoes, I do recommend you use the same pan on the stove top as in the oven; if you have to move the tomatoes out of the frying-pan and into a roasting pan, you will leave behind the delicious juices, and the cold new pan will slow down and affect the cooking process.
• As with most of my dishes, I recommend that you experiment, especially with sauces. Tomato Fondue, Antiboise Sauce, *Beurre Blanc* or Fish Velouté will all succeed with this recipe.
• In the restaurant, we might serve this in a pastry tartlet or with spinach and the tomatoes. Sometimes I like to see the fish cut into smaller pieces and served around a Central Salad page 178). Try the Vierge Sauce and tomatoes first, though: you will be delighted by the superb flavours.

Ceviche of Salmon
with mustard dressing

The flavours and presentation of this dish are simply brilliant for the summer. The dish provides a light, delicate and refreshing hors d'oeuvre and is easy to prepare.

Some of your guests might not be so keen on the dish if they knew it was not cooked, only marinated. Don't let them be put off by this fact: remember that smoked salmon is usually only lightly smoked and not cooked, and everyone likes it!

SERVES 4

For the ceviche:
250g boneless, skinless fresh salmon, cut in 1cm cubes
juice of 1 lemon
juice of 1 lime
chopped fresh tarragon
chopped fresh basil
chopped fresh dill
1 tablespoon white wine vinegar
1 tablespoon olive oil
200ml fromage frais
salt and pepper

For the dressing:
1 dessertspoon Dijon mustard
1 dessertspoon caster sugar
125ml extra virgin olive oil
chopped fresh chives (optional)
salt and pepper

1 Put the salmon in a large bowl and add the lemon and lime juice, chopped herbs, vinegar and seasoning. Stir together and add the olive oil.

2 Allow the mixture to marinate; it should turn opaque and start absorbing the citrus juices and the flavours of the herbs.

3 Mix the fromage frais with a touch of lemon juice to taste and some salt; do not mix it up too much or it will become too runny.

4 To make the dressing, simply blend the mustard and sugar with a whisk and add the olive oil and seasoning. Keep tasting – if you want to add a little vinegar you can – but don't overdo it because of the vinegar and citrus flavours in the ceviche mixture. Finally, add a few chopped chives, if you like.

5 After the salmon has marinated for at least an hour, use oiled metal pastry rings (about 7cm diameter) as moulds and fill them with the cubes of salmon. Compress and compact the fish mixture in the rings, until it holds its shape and sits 1cm lower than the top of the ring. Put the fromage frais on top and spread it with a palette knife, until smooth. Carefully remove the rings, so the ceviche stays in neat, circular shapes. Mix and pour the dressing around it (see Notes).

WINE A light, soft, slightly spicy wine, such as an Alsace Pinot Blanc.

Notes
• The key piece of equipment for this dish is a blow torch! When the ceviche is in the rings, blast it for one or two seconds only with the flame. This will ensure that the rings come away smoothly. If you haven't got a blow torch handy, you will just have to be careful how you slide the rings up and off. Grease them well beforehand.
• The top of the ceviche will need a little colour, so add a little Tomato *Concassé* and chervil to garnish, or use caviar or some chopped fresh herbs.

- To make excellent Tomato *Concassé*, quarter and de-seed a tomato. Press down on a tomato quarter and remove the skin, leaving a petal shape. (Tomato petals can also be used for garnishes.) Square off the petal top, bottom and at the sides. Then cut it across into three strips and in the other direction, into nine neat squares.
- The longer the mixture marinates, the more it cooks; it will keep for a day or so in the refrigerator but it may slightly toughen after this period.
- You can use double cream instead of fromage frais. Just whisk the cream gently while adding a little lime juice and seasoning. Whisk to soft peaks and it will be a perfect substitute (though the fromage frais is lighter and healthier).
- You could also serve this with a Circle Salad (page 178) or, and I urge you to try this, with Pickled Cucumber (page 138). It is delicious!

Rillette of Salmon

This is described here because we use it with Smoked Salmon Roulade (page 21) but it can be a dish on its own. It can be served moulded in a ring with a Circle Salad (page 178), with Pickled Cucumber (page 138) underneath, or moulded in plain pastry rings, topped with fromage frais, and the ring removed. It is delicious with Tapenade (page 9) on top, dressed with a vinaigrette of your choice.

It is easy to do, and ideal to prepare in advance. It is a great stand-by recipe, if you are short of ideas and want something that you know will succeed every time. I serve it a lot when I entertain and am a little short of time.

SERVES 6

450ml olive oil or equivalent of duck or goose fat
450g boneless, skinless salmon, cut in pieces of about 75g each
8 garlic cloves, halved
1 fresh thyme sprig
1 bay leaf
2 star anises
pinch of ground cloves
juice of half a lemon
salt and pepper

1 Warm the oil or fat very gently. Put the salmon into the warm oil, with all the other ingredients except the lemon juice. Poach on low heat until nearly cooked (probably about 10 minutes).
2 Remove the pan from the heat and allow to rest; it can rest for some time, but always allow at least 5 minutes to let the flavours infuse.
3 Remove the salmon very carefully and blend it with a little of the fat juices, with a wooden spoon in a bowl, until soft, yet still in coarse flakes. Make sure you don't get any of the whole herbs or spices in the mixture. Add the lemon juice and seasoning, taste and serve. I suggest moulding it first in a straight-sided metal pastry cutter, like the ceviche.

WINE A lemony wine like a Chablis or lightweight Chardonnay.

Notes
- The rillette is better when the fish has not been thoroughly cooked through. This helps keep it moist and succulent.

Warm Crab Gâteaux and Provençal Vegetables
with Thai ginger *beurre blanc*

This is a great dinner-party dish. It can be prepared in advance, as it holds well in the refrigerator, covered with a piece of foil and melted butter, which helps preserve the ingredients. The butter will melt, when re-heated, and will poach the dish.

When you serve this, the stack of vegetables topped with the neatly arranged courgettes glazed with butter looks very impressive. It is one of those dishes that looks as if you have gone to a lot more trouble than you really did. The round shape, coupled with the height, make a dramatic impact.

SERVES 4

For the gâteaux:
oil for frying
1 large aubergine, thinly sliced
250g white crab meat
6 plum tomatoes, sliced
fresh basil sprigs
2 courgettes, sliced thinly
100g butter, melted
salt and pepper

For the ginger beurre blanc sauce:
30ml white wine vinegar
60ml white wine
1 shallot, chopped
two 2cm cubes of Thai or fresh root ginger, peeled and chopped
250g unsalted butter, chilled and sliced
squeeze of lemon juice
salt and pepper

For the crab gâteaux:
1 Pan-fry the aubergine slices in a little oil for 2-3 minutes on each side, until golden.
2 Using straight-sided metal pastry cutters about 7cm in diameter, arrange alternate layers of aubergine, crab, tomatoes, basil (see the photo). Do this twice, to create alternate layers of vegetables and crab. Season each layer.
3 Blanch the courgette slices for 20 seconds and refresh them in cold water, before placing them on top. Brush a little melted butter on top of the stack of vegetables and cover with foil or baking parchment. Refrigerate until needed.
4 When required, preheat the oven to 180°C/350°F/Gas Mark 4. Season, and bake the gâteaux for about 10 minutes, until warm.

For the ginger beurre blanc sauce:
1 Follow the recipe for *Beurre Blanc* (page 110), reducing the vinegar, wine, fresh chopped ginger and shallots to a syrup. Then whisk slices of chilled butter into the reduction, piece by piece, until all the butter has been amalgamated and the sauce has the consistency of thin custard.
2 Pass the sauce through a sieve and add a squeeze of lemon juice. Season to taste.
3 Finely dice the remaining ginger and add it to the sauce at the end, for texture and extra flavour.

WINE Brilliant with a Pinot Grigio (Italian), which is slightly fresh, and palate-cleansing.

Notes
• Finishing this dish off is the final piece of artistry.
I suggest very finely chopped chives for colour, garnished with a few tomato petals (see photo).

Pot au Feu of King Scallops
with spinach linguine

I can't enthuse enough over this recipe – it is one dish that has received unanimous praise. Everybody loves it.

The secret here is the key ingredient – the king scallops. I am always looking for alternatives: lobster or crab claws also work well. If you can get them, you should always use dived king scallops. These are the most expensive type, but superb. You are paying for somebody to dive down and pick your scallops off the coral by hand: the alternative is a dredged scallop that has been dragged and banged around in a net. More than destroying the scallop, the dredging destroys the sea bed, which I don't approve of.

With dredged scallops, washing is vital. With dived scallops, the washing will be kept to a minimum, which is what you want. The flavour will not be washed out. Frozen scallops are available but tend to lack in flavour.

This dish uses a *nage*, which comes from the French *la nage*, which means 'swimming'. The *nage* is a juice that works well with the scallops and other shellfish, but is not made from fish itself. The exciting flavours of the *nage* will gently infuse the scallops as they poach slowly. There is an essential sweetness in this *nage*; it is delicious.

This dish should be served in large bowls. The idea is to leave the scallops half-covered by the *nage*. I have pan-seared them so they have a darker colour, making them stand out from the soup. The *nage* is very tasty; serve this dish with a fish knife and a spoon so your guests can drink it.

SERVES 4

12 king scallops, with coral removed
50ml oil
450ml scallop *nage* (see below)
85ml sweet wine (Muscat or Sauternes)
250g Spinach Pasta, made into linguine (page 174)
about 25g butter, melted
fresh tarragon sprigs, to garnish
fresh chervil sprigs, to garnish
chopped fresh chives, to garnish
salt and pepper

For the nage:
2 onions, coarsely chopped
1 leek, coarsely chopped
3 celery stalks, coarsely chopped
4 carrots, coarsely chopped
1 whole garlic head, cut in half horizontally
2 lemons, thickly sliced
1.5 litres cold water
6 black peppercorns
6 pink peppercorns
2 star anises
coriander sprig
tarragon sprig
230ml dry white wine

For the nage:

1 Put all the chopped vegetables and the garlic and lemon slices and spices into a large saucepan. Add the water and bring to the boil.

2 When boiling, add the herbs and spices. Remove from the heat and let the flavours infuse for a few minutes. Add the white wine.

3 Pour the mixture into a large, clean container and let all the flavours infuse for two days or so in the refrigerator.

4 When required, pass the *nage* through muslin through a sieve, discarding the solids.

For the scallops:

1 Pan-sear the scallops (three large ones or five small ones per portion) in a hot frying-pan, in the oil, until browned on one side, remove from the heat and drain on kitchen paper.

2 Warm the scallop *nage* in a saucepan, with the sweet wine. Taste and season it.

3 Warm the linguine in a saucepan, with a little boiling water and a small ladleful of melted butter. Season well and form into neat pasta towers (see page 174).

4 Poach the seared and drained scallops in the *nage* for about 4 minutes. Do not let the *nage* boil, because the scallops will over-cook and become rubbery.

5 Serve a tower of pasta in the centre of each large bowl. Pick the leaves off the sprigs of tarragon and chervil and sprinkle even quantities of the herbs around each pasta tower. Arrange three scallops in each bowl and pour over a quantity of the *nage*, to come half-way up each scallop. Serve with a soup spoon, so that your guests can drink the juices afterwards.

WINE A top-flight Sancerre, such as Henry Natter's, or a good Pouilly Fumé; also a sophisticated French white Burgundy, like Puligny Montrachet Premier Cru.

Notes

• The *nage* will keep for a week or so, with perfect results. It can also be frozen.

• I am sometimes uncertain about the origins of recipes. Different chefs at the Pink Geranium bring different ideas in and I am constantly reading books and talking to other chefs. In this case, however, I know that this recipe owes a lot to Marco Pierre White. It is his *nage* ingredients that I have adapted successfully.

Cheese and Tomato Straws

Cheese and tomato straws are a great favourite at the Pink Geranium, where we serve them on Sunday lunchtimes. They are light enough not to spoil anyone's appetite, but they do encourage diners to take another drink – ideal for the restaurant's bar! I like to serve them in the same bowl as a few black and green olives, dressed with a little olive oil. Today, you can buy olives dressed with Provençal herbs, which are superb.

This recipe has always been popular with children at parties, although I once used it, very successfully, for a Christmas reception for the vice-chairman of Tesco. This particular version is the one I used in my book *Only the Best*. Every Sunday morning, I would arrive at my restaurant to find another new copy of my book (we kept a stack in reception) lying open at this recipe, with a greasy thumb mark on it. I was flattered, but it was an expensive way for my chefs to check a recipe.

MAKES ABOUT 65

100g plain wholemeal flour
50g unsalted butter
75g Cheddar cheese, roughly grated
1 egg yolk
2-3 teaspoons cold water
2 tablespoons tomato purée

1 Preheat the oven to 230°C/450°F/Gas Mark 8. Sift the flour into a bowl and, using your fingertips, rub in the butter until the mixture resembles breadcrumbs. Stir in the cheese.
2 Blend together the egg yolk, water and tomato purée and add this to the flour mixture. Mix to a firm dough. You can keep this dough for a week in the fridge or for months in the freezer.
3 Turn on to a lightly floured surface and knead gently until smooth. Roll out thinly into a 25cm square; then cut into strips about 7 × 1 cm.
4 Place on a baking sheet and bake for about 10 minutes, or until golden. Leave to cool on a wire rack.

Notes

• The way to make these straws look interesting is to twist the thin strips of dough once or twice, before baking them. This lifts them from the ordinary. The cooking time is crucial, too: you need to keep checking the straws, because if overdone, they break up and taste burnt. Once they start to brown lightly, whip them out of the oven, cool and rest.
• In addition to tomato, you could also use fresh herbs, such as coriander, or perhaps Tapenade (page 9). A little lemon juice in place of 1-2 teaspoons of the water will also vary the flavour. Cheese and tomato straws are ideal for experimenting with various flavours of herbs, spices and seeds.

Soups

I used to feel fairly negative about soups. I had, somewhere in the back of my mind, the thought that they were second-class starters. I changed my opinion dramatically when I was working at the Savoy and was told: 'You can always judge a chef's ability by the quality of his soups'. I changed my thinking then and there.

A chef who produces an uninteresting or flavourless soup will, almost certainly, produce other courses in the same manner. I suppose the best advertisement I can give for soups is that I usually cook them when I am entertaining at home. Two particular favourites for my dinner parties are the Mediterranean Fish and Shellfish Soup and Mussel Soup with Orange and Basil.

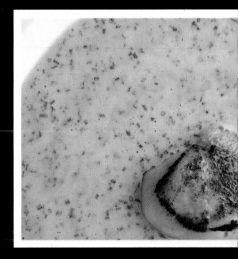

I think there are two routes to take, depending upon the occasion. Either decide what really special soup you want to produce and go for it. Or else consider what you have available and try to create a soup from those ingredients. As an example of the latter, I tried an onion soup which was simply mixed onions (spring, red, white and shallots), caramelized and mixed with vegetable stock. Served with bruschetta, it was wonderful.

Some of these soups use my basic stock recipes; you will find on pages 99-103.

Bread accompanies soup like vegetables to a main course, so do give some thought to some interesting breads to accompany these recipes (served warm, please!). I'd suggest chargriddled pitta bread dribbled with olive oil with the Mussel Soup, Ciabatta Bread with Gazpacho and homemade Tapenade Bread with the Mediterranean Fish and Shellfish Soup.

Manhattan Clam Chowder

'll never forget tasting this soup. It was when Sally and I were visiting friends in New York. We went to a wonderful oyster bar, just below Grand Central Station. It had every oyster you can imagine on sale, with glasses of champagne, Californian wine ... anything you could think of. It was full of people who were really into the food, especially shellfish. Their soup, the Manhattan clam chowder, was probably the best chowder I've ever had. Most importantly, the clams were very strong without being too fishy.

In addition to the chowder, the bread was excellent and the wine, by the glass, was superb too. I was really enjoying myself and told our host. He, with typical American openness and confidence, went off to tell the chef that 'a famous English restaurateur and writer' was praising his chowder. The chef, with whom we had a long chat, was very interested in what was happening in Britain and said, since I liked his chowder so much, that I could have the recipe. I have forgotten his name, so, if you're reading this, thanks, and please come to the Pink Geranium some time!

This is that recipe. It's very simple, with the secret, I think, in the amount of clams used. The only change I have made to the original is to add a little double cream. This reduces the emphasis of the butter and potatoes and helps to bring the whole dish together as a soup, providing a little more depth.

SERVES 4

75g pork back-fat, cubed
2 garlic cloves
1 onion, chopped
48 clams, cleaned
4 potatoes, peeled and cut in 1cm cubes
6 tomatoes, chopped
100ml white wine
125ml double cream
1 teaspoon fresh tarragon or chives, chopped
30g butter, chilled and cubed

1 Sauté the back-fat for 5 minutes, add the onion and garlic and heat until translucent and tender.
2 Add the clams, cover and steam for a few minutes, so the clams open. Then remove them and discard the shells.
3 Add the potatoes, tomatoes, wine and about 450ml of water and bring to the boil. Skim, reduce the heat and cook for 15 minutes. Liquidize and pass through a metal sieve. Add the cream slowly and reduce for 5 minutes.
4 Add the clams and leave them to simmer for a minute or two. Finally, whisk in the butter and the fresh herbs.

WINE Californian Fumé Blanc.

Notes
• You can leave out the cream, to try the recipe in its original form and to save a little money. Also, I remember enjoying the homemade bread and Californian wine on my visit, so perhaps you should ensure you have paid proper attention to these elements of your dish too.

Mediterranean Fish and Shellfish Soup

Mediterranean fish and shellfish soup is wonderful, warm and everything you'd expect a fish and shellfish soup to be. The flavours of the lemon grass, garlic, saffron and white wine really infuse into the liquid, to make this something rather special. The addition of the lobster sauce also adds greatly to the taste; the richness of it thickens and intensifies the flavours, although I should emphasise that it isn't crucial (see below).

One important secret is to cook the fish separately from the soup, bringing them together only at the last minute. Thus, each piece of fish is perfectly cooked.

SERVES 4

500g fresh live mussels in their shells
2 shallots, chopped
2 garlic cloves, crushed to a paste
pinch of saffron powder (optional)
pinch of cayenne pepper
2 lemon grass stalks, chopped
500g fish bones, chopped in small pieces
oil, for frying
125ml dry white wine
125ml water
250ml Lobster Sauce (page 106)
50g unsalted butter
pinch of salt
4 king scallops
1 red mullet, filleted, boned and cut in 4 portions
6 tiger prawns, peeled and cooked
chopped fresh basil

1 Scrub and wash the mussels, removing all barnacles and the beards.

2 Make a mussel stock, by sweating the shallots, garlic, saffron, cayenne, lemon grass and fish bones in a little oil and then adding the mussels. As the shells begin to open, pour in the white wine and then remove the pan from the heat and take out and reserve the mussels. Leave the bones and keep stirring.

3 Add the water, bring to the boil and skim occasionally. Simmer for approximately 1 hour.

4 Reduce this liquid by half and pass it through a sieve.

5 Now add the lobster sauce and butter, reduce again and taste; season.

To prepare the fish:

1 Pan-sear the scallops (page 29) and reserve them.

2 Fry the mullet until crisp, skin-side down first.

3 Poach the peeled prawns gently in the soup for a minute, just to warm them through, and add the mussels and the seared scallops.

4 Place a piece of red mullet in each soup bowl and serve the soup, evenly distributing the various fish between each bowl.

5 Add a little chopped basil and serve immediately.

 Provence Rosé.

Notes

• You can use many types of fish other than those listed; it isn't even essential that it is Mediterranean fish! You don't have to make a lobster sauce, either, but it does intensify the flavours and make the soup a lot richer and more concentrated. (You could just add a few lobster or prawn shells to the fish stock for simplicity.)

• If you are feeling really adventurous, a tower of fresh noodles (page 174) can be placed in the centre of each bowl, immediately before serving. Mediterranean fish and shellfish soup is very good served with Rouille as well (page 115).

Mussel and Orange Soup with Basil

The flavours of fresh mussels, orange and sweet basil are remarkably harmonious. This is an autumn and winter favourite at the Pink Geranium. In the summer, shellfish like lobster or scallops can be substituted for English mussels (which are only available when there is an 'r' in the month!).

Always be sure you buy mussels with tightly-closed shells; avoid those with broken shells (and discard any that have broken once you get them home). You will need to remove the mussel beard – the hair-like growth growing out of the shell; do this by pulling it down sharply to disconnect it. If you don't remove the beards, you may experience some tummy trouble!

SERVES 10

4 shallots, finely chopped
4 garlic cloves, crushed
vegetable oil
1350g fresh mussels, uncooked and in their shells, scrubbed and de-bearded
750ml dry white wine
500ml cold water
juice of 6 oranges
1 large bunch fresh basil
seasoning
250ml double cream

For the stock:
1 Make a mussel stock by sweating 2 chopped shallots and half the garlic with a little oil in a large saucepan until tender; add 900g mussels.
2 Stir well and allow the mussels to get hot. Add 500ml wine, with the water and orange juice. Bring to the boil.
3 Add some of the basil, to infuse the flavour into the stock, reduce the heat and simmer for 30 minutes.

4 Pass the stock through muslin or a fine sieve into a fresh saucepan. Discard these cooked mussels and retain the stock.

For the garnish:
1 In a little oil as before, sweat the other half of the garlic and shallots. Add the remaining cleaned mussels, and shake the pan. Stir well.
2 Add the last 250ml white wine. Bring to the boil once the shells of the mussels have opened.
3 Remove the mussels from their shells; discard the shells and reserve the mussels to add to the finished soup.

To finish:
1 Chiffonade (finely chop) the remaining basil.
2 Reduce the stock and add the double cream. Season to taste, but be careful not to add too much extra salt, as the mussels are fairly salty already. If absolutely necessary, add a little more orange juice.
3 When you are happy with the flavour, drop the garnish mussels into the soup and warm through. Add the basil and serve with a good pile of mussels in the centre of each bowl, pouring the soup carefully round it (see photo).

WINE
A limey Australian Riesling, such as Jane Mitchell's from the Clare Valley.

Notes
• Lime juice also works well, especially with coriander leaves instead of basil.

Smoked Haddock Soup

I have provided several different serving suggestions, as this is a soup that would go well as a starter for eight or make a good main course for a lunch for six, especially if served with the poached eggs (see below). Here is just the basic recipe … which is great in itself, of course.

This is an old favourite, a classic dish, and really easy to do. The cream and the milk poach the smoked haddock, which has such a strong taste that it cooks into the flavour of the soup. You don't really have to do much more than let it cook away and create its own flavour. If however you want a fuller fish flavour and you have my fish velouté (page 107) available, use this instead of the milk.

SERVES 6-8

1 onion, chopped
2 garlic cloves, chopped
50g unsalted butter
1 teaspoon curry powder
100ml dry white wine
300ml double cream, whipped
700ml milk (or fish velouté)
500g smoked haddock, skinned, boned and chopped
squeeze of lemon juice
salt and pepper

To garnish:
chives, chopped
garlic croûtons (optional)

1 In a large saucepan, sweat the onion and garlic for 5 minutes in the butter, until tender.
2 Add the curry powder and white wine. Cook for 2 minutes.
3 Add the whipped cream, milk and the fish and bring to the boil gently. Simmer for 15 minutes.
4 Liquidize and force through a fine sieve. Reserve.
5 To serve, bring back to the boil, taste and season. Add some lemon juice, taste, and serve with the chives and croûtons lightly distributed on the top.

A slightly oaky Chardonnay, like Kym Tolley's Penley Estate Chardonnay.

Notes

• I like to serve Smoked Haddock Soup with Rouille (page 115). If you do this, keep the croûtons to go with the dip. Another minor variation is to add a little freshly grated nutmeg to the soup.

• The big treat, if you are really ambitious, is to serve Smoked Haddock Soup with poached eggs. Simply poach the eggs, put one in the middle of the bowl and pour this wonderful soup around it. As you cut the egg with your spoon all the yolk runs into the soup – delicious!

• The secret is to cook the poached eggs in advance. Drop the eggs into your water (with a little vinegar to stabilise the whites of the eggs) and allow them to begin cooking, very gently. As the whites start to solidify, and you can see the yolks just starting to set, remove the eggs and put them immediately into iced water. This must be iced, which will stop the eggs cooking. The process also preserves the eggs exactly at this stage. When you want to use them, just drop them back into the boiling water for about 30 seconds and you've got perfect poached eggs every time. This allows you to get them ready for a dinner party well in advance.

• While on the subject of smoked haddock soup, I can't

resist suggesting another adaptation of this which is not really a soup at all. Try increasing the smoked haddock and taking out the milk completely; just add about 50ml of double cream instead. Cook this in exactly the same way and you will end up with a wonderful, thick, smoked haddock filling. This goes superbly in a pastry tartlet with spinach on the bottom, topped with a poached egg and maybe cheese sauce or Savoury *Sabayon* Sauce (page 105). Glaze this under the grill (or with a blow torch if you have one!) and you have a wonderful, exotic starter. You cut into the pastry, sabayon, poached egg and then into the haddock and the spinach ... it all works brilliantly.

Roast Parsnip Soup with Honey and Lemon

This was invented when I realised that the restaurant refrigerator was filling up with parsnip purée that had not been ordered to accompany a guinea-fowl dish. It is a wintry, thick soup that I have subsequently used for a golf club (where I am a consultant, not a player). The golfers always enjoy coming off the cold course to this thick, warming dish.

I mention the thickness, but don't overdo it. Use the cream and the stock to your taste, to produce a soup that has a substance but is not too creamy.

SERVES 4

For the parsnip purée:
850g parsnips, peeled and cut in medium cubes
juice of 2 lemons
3 heaped dessertspoons honey
sprig of fresh thyme
125ml olive oil

For the soup:
100ml double cream
100ml vegetable stock
pinch of freshly grated nutmeg
125ml dry white wine
salt and pepper
chopped fresh chives, to garnish

1 Mix all the parsnip purée ingredients and roast as described on page 176-177 but don't colour them more than light brown.
2 Blend the parsnips in a food processor until you have a fine purée.
3 Mix about a heaped dessertspoon of purée to 20ml of double cream per person. Thin with equal proportions of stock, to taste.
4 Finish the soup with nutmeg and some dry white wine. The soup should be thick but neither too heavy nor too creamy. Season well before serving and serve hot, with some chopped chives to garnish.

WINE Either a starchy white, like a white Rioja, or a light, silky red like Fleurie.

Notes
• Instead of the vegetable stock you could use a *nage* (page 28) if you have saved some. The dry white wine in that adds flavour and also aids thinning.
• Another variation which is also as delicious is curried parsnip soup – simply omit the lemon and add two dessertspoons of curry powder at stage 1. This will create a mild curry flavour which can always be adjusted to your liking at Stage 3.

Mushroom *Bouillon* with a Pan-seared Scallop

bouillon is a very light soup, almost a stock, but made with an essential extra ingredient, in this case mushrooms. This particular recipe has a strong mushroom flavour – but any good stock should have a blend of flavours. So here we have a great mixture of vegetables, with a strong influence of garlic as well.

You should think of this as a soup in two different parts. You are making the *bouillon* and a *liaison*, which is the cream and the egg yolk. These two come together at the last. The folding in of the *liaison* aerates the soup and helps make it light but creamy. You will end up with the flavours, not only of the mushrooms and vegetables but also the Madeira or sherry and, of course, the scallop.

SERVES 4

2 shallots, chopped
50g celeriac or fennel, chopped
1 celery stalk, chopped
1 small leek, chopped
2 garlic cloves, chopped
100ml olive oil
500g assorted mushrooms
50ml Madeira or dry sherry
1 litre vegetable stock or water
125ml dry white wine
4 king scallops
bunch of fresh tarragon
salt and pepper

For the liaison:
150ml whipping cream
4 egg yolks

1 Preheat the oven to 220°C/425°F/Gas Mark 7. Sweat the vegetables and garlic in a little olive oil until tender, but not coloured.
2 Slice the mushrooms and lay them on a baking tray; season and bake them for 10 minutes, to dry them out. Drying them in this way will increase their flavour considerably.
3 De-glaze the baking tray by adding a little Madeira or sherry to it and pour the mushrooms and all the juices into the saucepan with the vegetables. Cover with vegetable stock or water.
4 Bring the contents of the pan to the boil and skim, if necessary. After cooking for about 45 minutes, taste and liquidize well, until the mixture becomes finely textured, but thick.
5 Pass the mushroom soup through a very coarse sieve or colander so that the soup is neither too thick or too thin.
6 Put this mixture back into the saucepan and add a little more vegetable stock (if required) and the wine. Bring to the boil, taste and season.
7 Semi-whip the cream with the egg yolks; whisk together to form the *liaison*.
8 Sear the scallops on both sides and continue to cook them in the *bouillon* for a few minutes.
9 Add some chopped tarragon and fold in the *liaison*. Simmer very briefly and serve by putting a scallop into each bowl first and pouring the soup carefully around it.

WINE This is a grand soup, and suits a fine white Burgandy like Puligny Montrachet, or try a Maçonnais or Châlonnais.

(continued)

Notes

• Scallops and mushrooms may seem a funny combination but the scallop gives a wonderful contrast of flavour and texture. The scallop is seared and sits in the middle of the bowl and the soup goes around it, looks absolutely fantastic (see photo) and tastes beautiful. You need to serve it with a soup spoon and perhaps a fish knife and fork as well, for the scallop. The dish is very easy to prepare and, omitting the scallop, is a good vegetarian dish.

• You may not possess a coarse sieve (I don't!). What we use in the restaurant is a basket from a vegetable steamer. This gives about the right size of hole. Chip-basket holes are too large; those in a normal sieve are usually too small.

Crab Bisque

with lemon grass and ginger

Another fish soup, I know, but one so fantastic I just couldn't leave it out. It's perfect for autumn dinner parties, and my guests have even taken doggy-bags of leftover bisque home with them! Its rich flavour coupled with the creamy white crab meat really sets your palate alive. It's what soup should be all about.

SERVES 6

2 lemons, halved
2 large cock crabs (preferably alive), 900g-1350g each
4 tomatoes, cut into pieces
1 onion, roughly chopped
1 leek, roughly chopped
half head of celery, roughly chopped
2 large or 3 small garlic cloves
2 stalks lemon grass, chopped
cooking oil
600ml dry white wine
1 glass Armagnac (or cooking brandy)
about 2cm² fresh root ginger
150ml double cream
1 pinch freshly grated nutmeg
1 sprig fresh coriander, chopped
salt and pepper

To cook the crabs:

1 Drop the lemon halves into a large pan of boiling, salted water.

2 Plunge the live crabs into the boiling water, and cook until the water comes back to a rapid boil. This will take around 10 minutes with two crabs in the same pan.

3 Remove the crabs, and plunge them immediately into iced water to refresh.

To dress the crabs:

1 Remove the crab claws (cock crabs have larger claws, the females smaller) and crack as per lobster (see page 48-49), carefully using the back of a knife to remove the crab meat. Reserve the shells.

2 Using a strong knife, pry open the head to reveal the white meat on the under part. To remove, cut in half and pick out with a small pair of tweezers or a fish pick. Avoid the 'ladies' fingers' (see page 49), but reserve the shell.

3 Reserve the white meat to keep fresh in the refrigerator.

To make the soup:

1 Place all the shells on a baking tray; season and roast 20-30 minutes in a hot oven (230°C/450°F/Gas mark 8) until browned and crispy.

2 Meanwhile, prepare the stock by sweating off all the vegetables (except the ginger) in a large pan with a little cooking oil for about five minutes.

3 Add the white wine and simmer until the crab shells are ready; if this is going to take a while, add a little water to the stock mixture to prevent a reduction.

4 Add the crab shells to the stock pot, using half the brandy to deglaze the baking tray; add all juices to the stock pot.

5 Bring the stock to the boil; skim and simmer for about an hour until the stock has reduced by half. Taste; add more wine if necessary.

6 Pass the stock through a fine sieve into a clean saucepan; boil again to reduce by a third, adding the ginger. Taste and pass through a sieve a second time, to remove the ginger and prevent its flavour overpowering the soup.

7 Add the remaining brandy and bring back to the boil, then reduce the heat and add all except one tablespoon of the double cream; stir and season to taste.

8 While simmering the liquid, gently heat the crab meat with the remaining cream and season with nutmeg.

9 Serve by placing a portion of crab meat in the centre of the soup bowl, pouring the bisque around it. Dress the bisque with a little fresh coriander.

Notes

• Although it is best to cook your own crabs, many people prefer not to do this. You can buy pre-cooked or dressed crabs from your fishmonger or a good supermarket.

Gazpacho

There's gazpacho and there's gazpacho, and this is serious gazpacho. The addition of the green peppers along with the red peppers makes a little bit of difference and I also like the sliced white bread, put through the food processor with the soup, which provides extra thickening, and brings the flavours together more.

I used to make this soup, with almost the same recipe, when I was at the Savoy. The only difference was that we used mayonnaise instead of bread. That may seem strange but it added creaminess and flavour. Today, I prefer a more traditional, Spanish flavouring from the peppers, onion and garlic, finished with a bit of lemon juice and just thickened with the white bread.

SERVES ABOUT 12

2 green peppers, de-seeded and sliced, with one small slice finely chopped
5 red peppers, de-seeded and sliced
1 cucumber, peeled and de-seeded
about 25 tomatoes, peeled and de-seeded
1 onion
1 head of garlic
1 tablespoon white wine vinegar
4 slices of white bread, cubed, with crusts cut off
25ml lemon or lime juice, if necessary
small fresh basil sprig, finely chopped (optional)
1 tablespoon natural yoghurt or soured cream (optional)
chives, finely chopped (optional)
salt and pepper

1 Chop the vegetables and garlic roughly and liquidize them with the vinegar and bread.

2 When smooth, pass through a sieve (preferably nylon) into a clean container and then process and sieve again, to ensure a smooth finish. Chill.

3 Taste and add a squeeze of lemon or lime and serve. Alternatively, serve with a little chopped basil, a spoonful of natural yoghurt and some finely chopped chives.

A soft, easy drinking wine like Frascati, or a Viogner (from southern France).

Notes

• Caviar is also delicious with gazpacho; or serve the soup with the finely chopped condiments separately (e.g. peppers, cucumber, onion, shallots, etc.).

• You don't have to add the bread but it does give depth and brings all the ingredients into one.

Throughout this book, I emphasise the importance of using fresh food. Nowhere is this more important than with fish. Fresh fish contains so much more flavour and texture than fish that has been kept. Always try to find the freshest fish and cook it as soon as possible after you have bought it.

Generally, there are two types of fish available: those caught by trawler and those caught individually by fishermen. The former are often bruised and damaged: this is not surprising when you think that trawlers can catch up to 125 tonnes of fish at one go. The latter, unfortunately, are hard to come by and, as a consequence, often expensive. Also, in Britain, demand for unusual fish is low, so you are often restricted to a very limited variety.

Try to seek out good-quality fish, which often means those caught by local fishermen. If you have trouble obtaining any of the fish I have mentioned, please call my supplier, Direct Seafoods (01206 752075), the Sea Fish Industry Authority (0131 558 3331) or the National Federation of Fishmongers (0151 722 4059).

Consider the following pointers for spotting really fresh fish:

Smell:	light, pleasant and reminiscent of seaweed
Appearance:	shiny and slippery, with a metallic sheen
Scales:	strong, firmly attached to the skin (though fresh salmon often has missing scales)
Skin:	taut, deeply coloured, brilliant and adhering to the fish
Eyes:	clear, protruding and transparent
Gills:	moist, shiny and deep red or maroon
Flesh:	firm, translucent white or pink, with a sheen

One last important point about fish: never soak it in water. The flesh absorbs the water and this is detrimental to cooking. Simply wash fish inside and outside with cold water, to remove all traces of blood.

When choosing crabs or lobsters (crustaceans) or clams, scallops, etc. (bivalves), always buy them alive. Use them as soon as possible. If necessary, keep them wrapped in damp newspaper in the refrigerator for a short period only. Octopus, squid, etc. (cephalopods) should really be eaten immediately, although lobsters can survive a little while on the sea water in their shells.

Some of my fish recipes are quite complex, requiring careful preparation of the fish and, to set them off, very distinctive sauces and vegetables. What I always try to encourage, when cooking and teaching, is thinking ahead. In many cases, you can cook a part of the recipe and then reserve it, to finish the cooking just before serving. This is not the same as cooking and re-heating: the reserving stage will allow flavours to develop and blend and the second stage of heating will complete the cooking.

Importantly, this technique is good for entertaining. Recipes like Crisp-fried Fillet of Sea Bass, with baby spinach, confit of garlic and pesto dressing, or galette of John Dory, with ginger and spring onions and summer leaves sound impossibly complex, but break them down into stages and prepare what you can in advance and they are not. Your guests will be surprised how cool you are as you produce a range of exquisite and individual dishes.

Navarin of Fish and Shellfish
with a tarragon and Sauternes sauce and black pasta

A navarin, a sort of ragoût, is a great dish. We first thought of this particular *navarin* when we had lots of pieces of fish trimmed from other dishes to use up; it's colourful and tasty. The secret is in the way it is cooked: because you are cooking each part separately, you can control the flavours and the cooking fully.

The pasta is easy to make; don't be put off by the squid ink. It can be bought in sachets and you just pour it into the pasta. It comes out very black, but tastes really good.

Cooking fish can be quite difficult to control, as each type of fish cooks differently and at different times. Because this recipe has lots of different fish in it, the way it is cooked is really the secret, because you can control it by pulling the dish out of the oven every couple of minutes and taking it out straight away, as soon as it's cooked. This is more difficult to do if you're poaching, but you could bake some, poach some and griddle some, which would give the fish more of a variety of textures.

I have suggested using Fish *Velouté* Sauce (page 107) as an alternative to making the sauce. If you choose the *velouté*, follow that method, as it differs slightly from the one recommended here. Either way, add lots of chopped fresh tarragon to the sauce.

For dinner parties at home, I often do a mini *navarin* as a starter, with a piece of lobster, one scallop, a little salmon and halibut or sea bass.

SERVES 2

100g boneless, skinless halibut, halved
100g boneless, skinless salmon, halved
100g scallops
2 lobster claws
12 mussels

100ml vermouth
300ml dry white wine
2 sprigs fresh tarragon
2 cinnamon sticks
2 star anises

For the sauce:

2kg fish bones, shells from lobster or crab claws, etc.
5 garlic cloves, peeled and chopped
4 shallots, thinly sliced
2 leeks, chopped
1 fennel bulb, chopped
25ml olive oil
800ml water
500ml Sauternes or similar sweet wine
500ml double cream
small bunch of fresh tarragon
salt and pepper

For the pasta towers:

125g Pasta noodles (page 172)
2 sachets of squid ink

1 Line two small, flat baking tins (about 5cm deep and 25cm in diameter) with greaseproof paper. Arrange the fish in them, so that they do not touch each other or the sides. Pour over the vermouth and white wine (half to each tin) and add a tarragon sprig, cinnamon stick and star anise to each.

2 Cover the tins with tin foil, pierced at the top. Leave to one side while you prepare the sauce.

3 For the sauce, roughly chop the fish bones, using a meat cleaver or large chopping knife.

4 Sauté the garlic, shallots, leeks and fennel in the oil until tender, although not coloured. *(continued)*

5 Add the fish bones and shells and let them sweat for a moment, before adding the water. Leave to reduce slowly by about one third (this should take half an hour or so).

6 Add half the sweet wine. Allow to reduce a little and add the cream. Reduce again for about 10 minutes until it has the consistency of single cream.

7 Now add a few of the tarragon leaves, chopped, and the remainder of the Sauternes and leave to infuse. Strain through muslin into a clean container after 10 minutes. Finish the sauce with some more finely chopped tarragon and season it to taste. Use immediately once the last of the tarragon is added.

To cook the fish:

1 Preheat the oven to 200°C/400°F/Gas Mark 6. Bake the fish in the baking trays for about 10 minutes. Remove from the oven and check that the fish is cooked. Try not to over-cook it; it should be moist and gently baked.

2 Arrange the fish in a large bowl or on plates and pour the sauce over. Finish the dish with a tower of pasta and serve immediately (see photo).

WINE A good Sèmillon New World wine, or Alsace Pinot Blanc.

Notes

• You can use saffron in the sauce, which gives a wonderful contrast of yellow against the black of the pasta and the fish. Fresh saffron is expensive but you need only add a pinch to infuse the marvellous colour and flavour into the sauce. Add it to a little white wine and then pour the warmed wine and saffron into the creamy sauce and cook it; this helps to disperse the colour. Turmeric can also be used.

Whole Lobster
with *gremolata* and lime and ginger cream sauce

This is very much my own invention, mostly because I love *gremolata*. I used to enjoy *gremolata* sprinkled over *osso bucco*, a veal dish, but the unpopularity of veal means that we rarely cook this now. *Gremolata* is a mixture of chopped parsley and garlic with lemon zest and juice, usually sprinkled over as a garnish, although you can also use *gremolata* as a crust. It adds good flavours to fish or meat dishes and is ideal with lobster: in this recipe, it gives it a little bit of a kick. You can sprinkle it over the lobster, or put it on to whichever style of potatoes you choose to accompany the lobster; this looks prettier and neater (see photo). We would probably use it on the potatoes at the restaurant but there's nothing wrong with sprinkling it over the lobster at home; it's equally nice, especially if the lobster is served in the shell. I like to serve this on a bed of spinach.

Lobster works well with baby vegetables as it's such a delicate fish. The reason for serving it out of the shell is that it looks so attractive, and makes life so much easier for your guests. Don't get rid of the shells, however, as they can be used for making Lobster Sauce (page 106).

Importantly for entertaining, you can make this recipe in advance and then finish it off in the oven at the last minute.

2 lemons, halved
4 lobsters, weighing 600g-700g (live, if possible)
50ml dry white wine or fish stock
chopped fresh coriander
salt

For the gremolata:
large bunch of fresh parsley, finely chopped
3 garlic cloves, crushed
grated zest and juice of 2 lemons
salt

For the sauce:
125ml dry white wine
juice of 4 limes
5cm piece of fresh root ginger, peeled and finely chopped
200ml fish stock
200ml double cream
salt and pepper

To serve:
250g spinach
***Pommes Dauphinoise* (page 132)**
Deep-fried Leeks (page 169)

To cook the lobsters:
1 Drop the lemons into a large pan of boiling, salted water.
2 Plunge the live lobsters into the water and wait for the water to come back to the boil. When it's boiling, allow about 5 minutes for cooking the lobsters. Remove the lobsters, refresh them immediately in iced water and set them aside.

To make the gremolata:
Mix the parsley, garlic and the zest and juice of the lemons; season with salt and reserve.

To make the sauce:
1 Bring the wine to the boil with the lime juice and ginger in a large saucepan and leave to reduce to a thick glaze.
2 Add the cream and stock and reduce again to the consistency of single cream; season and reserve.

To dress the lobster:
1 Remove the lobsters from the water and carefully cut them in half, using a sharp knife, from the underneath of each lobster (where the little legs are – see photos). Carefully remove the tails.

2 Twist off each claw and, using the back of a heavy knife, crack them open and remove all the meat.

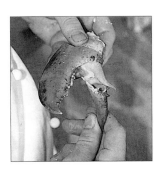 

3 Now arrange the tails and claw meat together as a portion and put them all in a baking dish or tray. At this point, the lobsters could be set aside until you are ready to finish cooking them.

To finish:

1 When appropriate, preheat the oven to 200°C/400°F/Gas Mark 6. Pour the dry wine or fish stock over the lobsters and season them.

2 Add a little chopped coriander, cover the dish with foil and bake for about 6 minutes, until the lobster is hot and cooked through. Add the poaching wine/stock to the sauce before serving.

3 Serve each portion of lobster on a bed of spinach (page 175). Cut perfect rounds of *Pommes Dauphinoises* with a straight-sided metal pastry cutter, arrange on the plate and sprinkle with the *gremolata*. Make a tower of the Deep-fried Leeks to give some height. Pour the sauce around.

WINE A rich Meursault (Burgundy white) or Puligny Montrachet.

Notes

• This dish is also delicious with a Lobster Sauce (page 106) or any other fish sauce, if you want, leaving out the lime and ginger, although you would still use the *gremolata*. Lobster Sauce makes good use of the lobster shells!

• The potential variations on this dish are numerous. It is particularly nice with baby vegetables and asparagus works very well, too. Or try *Pommes Fondantes* (page 132) with the *gremolata* on top of each one. There's plenty of choice.

Crisp-fried Fillet of Sea Bass
with baby spinach, *confit* of garlic and pesto dressing

Sea bass is very popular; it's probably Great Britain's premium fish. It is meaty and full of flavour, and is Sally's and my favourite. Make sure, however, you buy it very fresh; it loses its quality very quickly. This recipe has wonderful Mediterranean flavours and makes an attractive dish, with lots of lovely colours, served with baby vegetables and baked garlic.

As the title suggests, it is important that the fish is crisp. This is achieved by cooking it in a hot pan and serving it with the skin on. The secret of the crisp skin is pressing down on the fish in the pan as it cooks.

Another point of interest in this recipe is the garlic *confit*. This is a great way of cooking garlic: almost poaching it in wine, butter and herbs, which softens and sweetens it, mellowing the harsh flavour of raw garlic. It's a wonderful accompaniment to the fish. I recommend about three cloves per person.

For the sea bass:
1kg (or slightly less) sea bass, preferably cut from a fish of about 3kg, cut in 200g fillets
plain flour, seasoned
oil, for frying

For the sauce:
125ml extra virgin olive oil
2 heaped dessertspoons Pesto Sauce (page 115)

For the spinach:
60g unsalted butter
450g spinach leaves, washed and stalks removed
freshly grated nutmeg
salt and pepper

To serve:
12 whole cloves *Confit* of Garlic (page 170)
chopped fresh chives or coriander (optional)
Char-griddled New Potato Slices (page 131) or *Pommes Fondantes* (page 132)
Baby Vegetables (page 177), e.g. mange-tout peas, baby leeks and fennel

1 Preheat the oven to 200°C/400°F/Gas Mark 6.

2 Coat the fillets with flour and pat to remove any excess.

3 In a hot frying-pan, heat the oil and fry the fish fillets, skin-side down first. Press down on the fillets with a kitchen cloth, so that they do not curl up (after a minute they will stay flat). After a few minutes (when the fish is golden brown on the skin side) turn it over and cook the other side.

4 Remove the fish from the pan and finish it in the oven for 7-10 minutes.

5 Warm the olive oil and whisk in the pesto. Do this just before serving, to preserve the green colour of the pesto. Taste and season the sauce.

6 Take a fresh frying-pan and add a little oil and the butter; fry the spinach until it wilts and add a little nutmeg and salt to taste. Drain on kitchen paper and serve in the centre of the plate, in a neat circle.

7 Now put the crisp sea bass, skin-side up, on the spinach and pour the sauce around. Garnish with the garlic *confit* and chopped chives or coriander. Arrange the potatoes, and add the vegetables. *(continued)*

Premier Cru Chablis.

Notes

• This recipe can be used for other fish, such as red mullet, as a starter, or even cod or halibut.

For fanned fondant potatoes:
• Turn the potatoes into barrel shapes and slice off the bottom so that they stand flat. Now carefully slice thinly through each potato at a slight angle. Braise the potatoes in a little stock and water (covered with tin foil as per fondant potatoes, page 132) until tender. Remove the potatoes from the stock and glaze under a hot grill to serve.

Poached Oysters in Champagne

This is a recipe we've used in the restaurant as a starter. I think many people prefer to eat oysters when they have been cooked, but only gently. Over-cooking makes them rubbery and ruins the delicacy of this dish. Softly poached, they absorb all the flavours of the champagne and the *sabayon*.

Ideally, you should serve this with a little caviar. I suggest Sevruga or Ossetra, both of which should be a little cheaper than the favoured Beluga. Oysters, champagne and caviar? Yes, OK, this is rather a decadent dish and I'm not suggesting cheaper alternatives. If you are going to push the boat out, do it in style. See page 43 for my serving recommendation.

The recipe is fairly straightforward and easy to prepare, but looks very exotic on the plate. One tip for presentation is to serve an odd number of oysters per portion; odd numbers look better on the plate than even. Better still, see if you can get some seaweed from the fishmonger; put this on the base of the plate, with the oysters in the shells on top. You might want to add half a lemon wrapped in muslin to the finished dish. The muslin ensures that when you squeeze the juice over the oysters, it goes over the oysters and not over you.

SERVES 2

10 fresh oysters
125ml champagne
90ml Savoury *Sabayon* Sauce (page 105)
2 teaspoon Sevruga or Ossetra caviar
half a lemon or lime, cut in half

1 Open the oysters with your oyster knife, with the deep part of the shell downwards, to reserve the juices (see photos). Pass the juices through a fine sieve into a saucepan and clean out the shells.

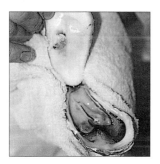 

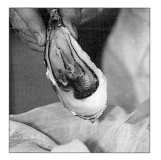 

2 Pour the champagne into the oyster juices and gently poach the oysters for a maximum of 45 seconds; remove the oysters.

3 Warm the oyster shells under the grill (or in the oven) and prepare the *sabayon*.

4 Put the oysters into the shells, top with the *sabayon* and glaze under a hot grill for a few seconds or use a blow torch. Garnish with the caviar and serve.

WINE Champagne!

Notes

• You could add a sprig of fresh chervil with the caviar or put a little linguine pasta under each oyster for added flavour.

• While we are thinking about oysters, I ought to mention another idea for a similar starter. This uses the oysters cold, topped with a lemon cream (double cream, lemon juice and a pinch of salt, gently blended). Each oyster is served with a small amount of the lemon cream, topped with caviar. This is simpler and, without the champagne, a little cheaper.

John Dory Fillets
with potato galettes, tomato fish sauce and baby vegetables

John Dory is an excellent fish, although it may not always be easy to obtain. I think of it as a very English fish so I have structured the rest of the recipe to reflect this.

The sauce is a blend of Tomato Fondue and Fish *Velouté*, which work wonderfully together. The textures are good, the garnish of the galette of crisp potato and spinach is superb and the baby vegetables in the sauce add colour and interest. The construction of the dish is quite easy and the overall effect is magnificent. This dish, like many others in this book, reflects my preference for round and tall construction.

I realise that this recipe demands that you skip around the book a great deal, to find all that you need. I think it's worth it. Looked at positively, this demonstrates how you can construct a great wealth of interesting recipes of your own, simply by combining a range of basic elements.

SERVES 4

600g John Dory fillets, skinned
100g plain flour, seasoned
100ml cooking oil
salt and pepper

For the sauce:
125ml Fish *Velouté* Sauce (page 107)
250ml Tomato Fondue (page 109)
salt and pepper

To serve:
12 Potato Galettes (page 90)
300g spinach (page 175)
selection of Baby Vegetables (page 177)

1 Preheat the oven to 200°C/400°F/Gas Mark 6. Coat each fillet of fish with flour and shake it well, to ensure it has only a light coating.

2 Fry the fish in a frying-pan, in very hot oil, on both sides, until crisp and brown. Remove the fish and let the fillets rest.

3 Prepare the Tomato Fondue and Fish *Velouté* sauce.

4 Blend the two sauces, so they are intermingled but still retain hints of their individuality. Season to taste.

5 Make about a dozen galettes. Prepare the spinach and the baby vegetables.

6 Finish the fish in the oven for 5 minutes.

7 Construct layers of potato galettes, spinach and fish, surrounded by a pool of the creamy tomato sauce, with the baby vegetables placed around it (see photo).

WINE Australian Sèmillon or Chardonnay.

Notes

• The addition of some pan-fried wild mushrooms (try chanterelles or trompettes) would also be nice but might make the plate look a little too busy. The mushrooms could, possibly, replace the baby vegetables in this case. If you wanted to use them, make sure you de-glaze the frying-pan by adding a little white wine and stirring before seasoning and serving the mushrooms, so you don't lose any of their delicious juices.

• On the topic of substitution, you could use plain double cream to blend with the Tomato Fondue, instead of the *Velouté*, for a simpler version.

Escalopes of Salmon
topped with mozzarella and served with a fish *velouté*

This recipe was first made in the restaurant by one of my head chefs and it used to appear on the lunch menu. It was his idea to cut the salmon into small, elongated triangular shapes, thick at one end and thin at the other. This tapering created a pizza shape, when arranged in a circle on the plate, thin ends towards the centre. The sauce and scattered vegetables, herbs and cheese reinforces this, especially since they cook together at the last. I always take care to keep the salmon slightly pink; the ideal way to enjoy the fish.

I think I introduced this chapter with a warning note about fresh ingredients. This recipe is the exception to the rule! You will find that canned tomatoes are as good, if not better, for this tomato sauce than fresh tomatoes.

SERVES 4

1 teaspoon olive oil
900g boneless, skinless fresh salmon
100g button mushrooms, finely sliced
4 tomatoes, skinned, de-seeded and chopped
225g mozzarella cheese, finely sliced
30g fresh chives, chopped
30g tarragon

For the tomato sauce:
15g unsalted butter
8 shallots, chopped
12 fresh basil leaves
1 tablespoon tomato purée
425g canned chopped tomatoes
60ml white wine
salt and pepper

To serve:
250ml Fish *Velouté* Sauce (page 107)

1 Preheat the oven to 230°C/450°F/Gas Mark 8. For the sauce, melt the butter and cook the shallots and half the basil until the shallots are transparent. Add the tomato purée, canned tomatoes and white wine; reduce this mixture until it is a thick sauce. Pass the sauce through a fine sieve, season it and leave it to cool.

2 Cover a baking tray with greaseproof paper and brush the greaseproof with olive oil. Cut the salmon into triangles and arrange them on the greaseproof in four circles, with the thicker sides outwards (to resemble a pizza). Season the salmon and then spoon on the tomato mixture.

3 Scatter the mushrooms, tomatoes, tarragon, basil, mozzarella and chives on top. Bake for 10 minutes. Place in the centre of the plate. Serve with the *Velouté* Sauce.

WINE Slightly chilled light red, like Chirables, or a Pinot Noir.

Notes
• This recipe also works well with Savoury *Sabayon* (page 105) instead of the *Velouté* Sauce, giving another variation. In this case, pour the *sabayon* on the plate, glaze it with a blow torch or under the grill and then arrange the salmon on top.
• I haven't suggested vegetables with this one, because it is a busy dish. You could add vegetables and potatoes but I would recommend a Caesar or Niçoise salad. Served with a salad, it is an excellent light course, especially on a summer evening. A smaller version of this could also make an excellent starter.

Char-griddled Fresh Tuna Steak
with ginger, spring onions and summer leaves

There is a tendency to rely upon vegetables and potatoes to accompany main course dishes. I can understand this – and it doesn't mean the food will be dull – but it's good to break away from this pattern whenever possible. Fish, for example, is excellent served on dressed salad leaves. I have suggested a range of leaves in the ingredients list but see what is around and try out different types.

The key to this recipe is the use of fresh tuna, which is more readily available now; it is so much better and 'cleaner' in taste than canned tuna. When marinated, it absorbs all the flavours and it tastes superb when char-griddled. The ginger and spring onions make this dish a little bit oriental and absolutely superb.

Char-griddling creates a Mediterranean flavour and I think this should be reflected in the presentation of the dish. Create a small circle of leaves, with the ginger and spring onions in the centre, or use a loose, tossed salad, with tomatoes and onions falling from the sides, and put the tuna on top.

Serve with baked new potatoes in their skins (and plenty of salt), or a bowl of pasta.

SERVES 4

800-900g fresh tuna loin, sliced about 1cm thick
olive oil
2cm piece of fresh root ginger, peeled and thinly sliced
bunch of spring onions
100g unsalted butter, plus a little extra to serve
150ml dry white wine
salt and pepper

For the salad and dressing:
olive oil
sherry or balsamic vinegar
finely chopped fresh chives (optional)
selection of summer leaves, e.g. rocket, lollo rosso, radicchio, oak-leaf, frisée and dandelion, rinsed and dried
salt and pepper

For the marinade:
2 garlic cloves, crushed
large sprig of fresh coriander
about 12 black peppercorns
juice of 1 lemon
olive oil
salt and pepper

1 Preheat the oven to 230°C/450°F/Gas Mark 8. Bring all the marinade ingredients together and season to taste, before adding the slices of tuna.
2 In a very standard heavy-duty frying-pan, fry the ginger in a little olive oil, until tender. Then add the spring onions, butter and white wine. Cook this until the juice has almost evaporated and season to taste.
3 Make the dressing by mixing two parts of olive oil to one part balsamic vinegar; season and add the chives (if using). Pour the dressing over the leaves and toss well.
4 Arrange the salad in the centre of the plate.
5 While the spring onions are still cooking, griddle the tuna steaks on both sides until you have a 'griddle mark', if you're using a char-griddle pan, or a crisp, brown coating if using a frying-pan.
6 Remove the tuna from the heat and finish it in the oven for about 5 minutes, depending on the thickness of the steaks (the 1cm I have suggested is a good thickness). *(continued)*

7 Serve the gingered spring onions in the centre of the circle of salad and put the tuna steak on top. Brush the top with a little melted butter, to give it shine and finish.

A good white Australian Riesling.

Notes

• You could use swordfish or shark in the same way but I highly recommend the tuna. It is definitely worth experimenting with this fish; it's so delicious and more like a meat in texture.

• If you don't find the salad leaves you require, try the tuna with a Niçoise-style salad; the black olives, green beans and so on make an ideal accompaniment.

Main Courses with Meat, Poultry and Game

I normally see these non-vegetarian main courses as set pieces, works of art for the restaurant: the way in which the Pink Geranium will be remembered by our clients. For you, they will probably form the centrepiece of an evening's entertaining, and I hope, your conversation!

First a word about ingredients: no recipe idea, no matter how delicious and original, will be successful if the main ingredient – in this case the meat – isn't good enough quality. For red meat (and also for game) this means that, in addition to being carefully reared, it must be well hung. The idea of hanging meat seems to be in danger of becoming an historical curiosity. The process, which induces weight loss, is just not economical for butchers, who already face difficult EC regulations. I'm afraid this means that you will be buying meat that is simply too fresh. Bright red meat means not hung, not mature and generally tough to eat; deep red meat means well hung, well matured and deliciously tender. I choose to hang my own meat whenever possible, including game and poultry. Don't expect anything to be hung, unless you do it yourself.

In general, when choosing a main course, I think first of the season. This strongly influences my selection of meat: venison and game in winter; spring lamb; poultry for summer. Then I consider the sauces and vegetables and the ways they complement the meat: through taste, colour and texture. In both aspects of a recipe – the meat and the accompaniment – I will go for my best option. If that is difficult, because of missing ingredients or lack of time, I will search for alternatives. This is what you should do. If you don't have time for one type of potato dish, choose another. If you prefer baby vegetables to roasted vegetables, use them. If you are short of veal *jus*, use some other stock.

Don't be put off trying one of these recipes because of one or two missing ingredients: improvise or substitute instead. Also, do not be put off by the apparent complexity of the recipes. Some of these could go in the Twenty-minute Marvels chapter, although some take much longer, and most allow opportunities for getting used to mise en place: preparing foods well in advance of the final cooking.

A note on meat

Since the scares about BSE I have been buying my meat from an organic farm in Scotland. The Aberdeen Angus I now buy is much more expensive than other beef available, but I do feel that the quality of meat produced by intensive methods has deteriorated in recent years, and I also have an obligation to my clients. All the scaremongering apart, I do also feel the intensive methods now used for mass-produced meat have diminished its flavour and quality. While the British beef trade has suffered terribly with the BSE issue, I hope that with the end of controversial feeding practices we can also see a more general change of approach in meat production. Consumer power has been shown to be very important: with more public demand, organic products will become more widely available, and likewise hanging too.

If you have any queries about meat, please don't call me! Call the Meat and Livestock Commission (01908 677577). You can also obtain information about your nearest organic meat supplier from the British Organic Farmers Association in Bristol (01179 299666). For £3.00 and an SAE sent to 86-88 Colston Street, Bristol BS1 5BB, they will send you their booklet of British organic meat and vegetable suppliers. Cambridge and Smithfield Meat Services (0171 248 3007) are my butchers, and can advise you on the availability of specialist meats.

Loin of New-season Lamb
with baked peppers, garlic juices and char-griddled vegetables

When I think of a recipe, I think of the season we are in and what are the best ingredients at the moment, how the marriages of these flavours will be and, finally, the colours and presentation of the dish. This dish does it all. Apart from looking seriously stylish, it optimizes fashionable Mediterranean flavours.

I use this at the Pink Geranium, especially in the spring, with new-season lamb, which doesn't have very much fat. In the south of Britain, it's normally available in the shops in April and May; at the restaurant we might get it a bit earlier. Loin, of course, is the leanest cut but it still has some fat, which we do leave on while cooking.

What I would do a couple of days before cooking this is pull the fat away from the meat, bat out the fat a little with a rolling pin and then season the meat with salt, pepper and little olive oil and some freshly chopped herbs (mint or coriander would work well). Then I would roll the loin of lamb in the fat, tie it tightly into a cylindrical shape and wrap it in cling film. This will benefit from being left in the refrigerator for a day or two. It will grow in flavour and keep its shape well during cooking. Alternatively you can just roll the loin (see photos) and refrigerate, for speed and simplicity.

An important aspect of cooking the lamb is letting it rest afterwards; this allows you to judge how it is cooked. If you were preparing this in advance for a dinner party, cook it rare and allow it to rest; then you can cook it to medium-rare or medium, depending on which you prefer, when you need to serve it.

SERVES 4

1 green pepper
1 yellow pepper
1 red pepper
25ml olive oil
1 loin of lamb, off the bone, cut into portions of 3-4 cutlets
    each, weighing about 200g each when fat removed
450ml lamb stock, made from the bones, or Veal *Jus*
    (page 100)
2 garlic cloves, chopped
175ml red wine
salt and pepper

To serve:
selection of Mediterranean Vegetables (page 180),
    e.g. courgettes, aubergines
Rösti Potatoes (page 130), optional

1 Preheat the oven to 230°C/450°F/Gas Mark 8. Pan-sear the peppers until they are almost black all over. Then bake them in the oven for 10 minutes, until soft and tender. Put the peppers in a bowl and cover them quickly with cling film. This will create a near vacuum, which will cause the skins of the peppers to start to fall off, making them easier to peel.
2 Pan-fry the lamb loins in the hot olive oil on both sides until browned. Then roast them for about 8 minutes for medium-rare meat. The lamb should, ideally, be pink, so after 8 minutes remove it from the oven and allow it to rest on a cooling rack for 10 minutes or so.

3 The sauce is made from a natural stock. Reduce it to the consistency of single cream and pass it through a muslin-lined sieve, to remove all particles. Pour the stock into a clean saucepan and add the red wine and the garlic. Cook for a further 10 minutes, to allow the flavours to infuse. Pass through a clean fine sieve or tea strainer again, to remove the garlic cloves.

4 Peel and slice the peppers, removing the seeds, and add them to the sauce; taste the sauce and season accordingly.

5 Put the loins of lamb back in the hot oven to warm through. Meanwhile, char-grill the Mediterranean vegetables.

6 Remove the string and slice the lamb into thin strips. Arrange these in a circle in the centre of the plate, perhaps on a rösti potato. Serve the sauce by carefully pouring it around the lamb. Scatter the vegetables in a circular fashion over the plate.

WINE Californian Merlot, or a Bordeaux such as Pomerol or Margaux.

Notes

• This is a pretty dish to look at. It could also be served on a risotto of wild mushrooms, arranged in a ring, with the lamb fanned on the top. It works well with several other sauces, including garlic cream sauce.

• A favourite alternative is to serve it with Garlic *Beignets* (page 138) but you will probably need to be a garlic fanatic to have this much garlic together!

Breast and Thigh of Free-range Chicken
in its own *confit*, with *saladaise* potatoes, wild mushroom sauce and Madeira *jus*

Some of the most wonderful-sounding dishes are actually very easy to prepare: very often, you can tackle a quite complex recipe fairly easily, by breaking down the method into separate parts. This is one such example, where each part is easy; together they look and taste exceptionally good.

In this recipe, we use a *confit* of chicken thighs. The main secret of cooking all game birds or poultry successfully is not to cook the thighs and breasts for the same length of time. The tougher fibres in the legs need to be more broken down, as they are quite chewy, whereas the breast only needs to be cooked lightly.

Cooking the thighs this way gives a number of serving options. You can take the meat off the bone and mix it in with the potato; alternatively, serve it on the potato and put the breast on top. Either way, it's a nice combination of flavours: the chicken breast tastes roasted and the thigh has all the wonderful flavours of a *confit*. This is a superb dish for flavours, with the poultry cooked to perfection.

(continued)

2 medium-size, free-range chickens
oil, for frying

For the confit:
800g duck or goose fat or cooking oil
1 head of garlic, cut in half horizontally
peel of 1 orange
small piece of fresh root ginger
sprig of fresh thyme
salt and pepper

For the saladaise potatoes:
3 large (baking) potatoes
115g unsalted butter
potato flour (if necessary)
salt and pepper

For the sauce:
250ml Veal *Jus* (page 100) or chicken stock
450g fresh wild mushrooms, or, out of season, dried
150ml dry Madeira
25ml cooking oil
salt and pepper

To serve:
French beans (page 175), Glazed Carrots (page 175) and
asparagus, if in season (page 177)

For the confit:
1 Preheat the oven to 150°C/300°F/Gas Mark 2-3. Remove the legs of the chickens and then cut through the legs, to remove the drumsticks (see photos **a** and **b**).

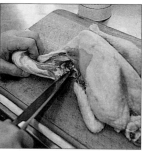

a   b

2 Warm the duck or goose fat or oil in a baking tray, add all of the *confit* ingredients and then the chicken thighs. Cover with foil and bake for about 2 hours.
3 Whilst this is cooking, sprinkle the potatoes with a little salt and bake them for about 1½ hours, or until they are soft and tender.

For the sauce:
1 Reduce the veal *jus* or chicken stock by about a third.
2 Add the dried mushrooms, if using, and leave to simmer, to allow the flavours to infuse. If you are using fresh mushrooms, reserve them until the end of the recipe.

For the potatoes:
1 When the potatoes are cooked, remove the skins and blend in about 125ml of the *confit* fat from the tray. Mix well, season and refrigerate, which will make the texture more firm.

2 When the potato mixture is cold, mould it into four cakes in 8cm plain pastry rings. Either fry them in some of the *confit* fat until they are crisp and brown or bake them in the oven. You may need to add a little potato flour at this stage, if the mixture is still wet.

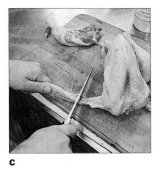

c

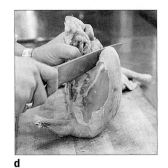

d

e

f

g

h

To finish:

1 Remove the chicken breasts from the carcass (see photos **c-h**). Fry them in hot oil until golden brown. Finish in the oven, by roasting for about 7 minutes, depending on the size of the breasts.

2 Meanwhile, finish the sauce by adding the Madeira to the reduced stock. Lightly fry the fresh mushrooms in a little oil. Drain them on kitchen paper and add them to the sauce. Allow the sauce to simmer for a further 5 minutes or so, to allow the flavours to infuse and season.

3 After 2 hours, remove the chicken thighs from the *confit*. The thigh bone should fall away from the flesh easily, indicating that it is cooked to perfection.

4 Arrange the potato cakes in the centre of the plate and then put the chicken thigh on top and lean the breast on top of the thigh. Pour the sauce over the top, ensuring that some of the mushrooms fall over the top of the chicken. Garnish with crisp green French beans, glazed carrots and tiny spears of asparagus, if it's available.

WINE A lightish Burgundy, such as Savigny les Beaune.

Notes

• You can use all kinds of wild mushrooms, such as chanterelles, girolles, *pieds de mouton*, or even shiitake mushrooms. If using dried mushrooms ensure they are well cooked in the sauce because they will be chewy; pass the sauce through a sieve before you serve it, which will give you the flavour of the mushrooms without the pieces.

• Cook the drumsticks left over from this recipe in the leftover *confit* fat in the same way. Remove the meat from the bones, mince it and use it to make a *rillette* of chicken. This can then be used in the same way as Salmon Rillette (page 25); spread it on croûtes for canapés or mould it in a pastry cutter like the Chicken Gâteaux (page 14).

Steven's famous Pink Geranium Crispy Duck
with caramelized apples, Calvados *jus* and roasted parsnips

This recipe goes back several years and actually started out as a mistake. I'd put ducks in the oven, fortunately on a very low heat, and completely forgot about them until about 2½ hours later – about an hour longer than I would normally have left them. The ducks, however, were still tender and moist and the skin wonderfully crisp. It was served in the restaurant and people complimented me on it; some said it was the best duck they'd ever tasted!

People, generally, do like their duck well cooked. It's only chefs and really foody people who like duck pink. If a chef undercooks something, he'll tell you that is the way it's meant to be; but he'll be worried about over-cooking because somehow that seems to demonstrate a lack of skill. The real skill, of course, is in cooking meat and poultry just right, and just how people enjoy eating them. So we have carried on serving duck cooked my way, varying only the sauce each season.

This is a good autumn dish, with the contrast of the savoury duck and the sweetness of the apples and parsnips. It's quite a rustic-looking dish too, which I like. It needs some simple green vegetables, such as beans or spinach, to accompany the parsnips and a simple potato dish, such as Mashed Potatoes (page 131) or *Pommes Fondantes* (page 132).

This also works well if you use summer fruit, blackberries and so on instead of the apples, maybe with some *cassis* in the sauce.

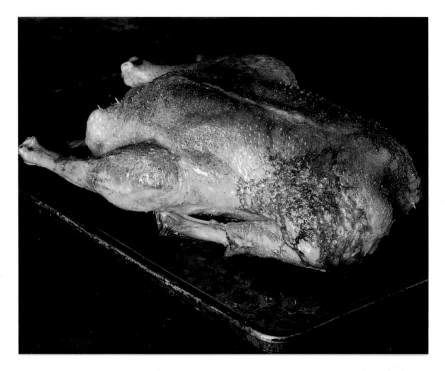

SERVES 4

2 large English ducks, weighing about 2kg each
bunch of fresh thyme
selection of English seasonal vegetables, roughly chopped to a *mirepoix*
salt and pepper

For the caramelized apples:
6 English Cox's or similar eating apples, peeled, cored and sliced
50g unsalted butter

75g sugar
75ml white wine vinegar
100ml white wine
icing sugar (optional)

For the sauce:
300ml Veal *Jus* (page 100) or chicken stock
60ml Calvados
60g unsalted butter, chilled and cut in pieces
salt and pepper

For the parsnips:
4 small parsnips, peeled
150ml olive oil
1 dessertspoon dried thyme
1 tablespoon honey
salt and pepper

To serve:
selection of green vegetables, Mashed Potatoes (page
131) or *Pommes Fondantes* (page 132)

To cook the ducks:
1 Preheat the oven to 150°C/300°F/Gas Mark 2-3. Trim ducks by removing part of the wing bones and wishbones.
2 Season the birds inside and out and put them in a deep roasting tray, with the roughly chopped vegetables.
3 Roast for a little over 2 hours, occasionally pouring the fat from the baking tray.

For the caramelized apples:
1 Sweat the apples in the butter and then add the sugar, vinegar and wine and cook until tender but not mushy.
2 Alternatively, liberally dust the slices of apple with icing sugar and simply grill or bake them, until brown and tender. The first method gives more complexity of flavour but the second is far simpler and quicker.

To make the sauce:
1 Reduce the *jus* or stock by a third. Taste it and season.
2 Add the Calvados and reduce again, for about 5 minutes.
3 Check the seasoning again. Whisk in the butter, a piece at a time, to thicken and enrich the sauce. Taste again.

To cook the parsnips:
Turn the oven up to 220°C/425°F/Gas Mark 7. Cut the parsnips into small batons and toss them in enough olive oil to coat them. Add the dried thyme and then the honey and seasoning and mix in well. Roast in the oven for about 15 minutes, or until crisp and brown.

To serve:
1 Turn the oven up to 230°C/450°F/Gas Mark 8-9. Finish cooking the ducks, crispening and browning them for about 30 minutes.
2 Remove from the oven and allow to rest for 5 minutes, before carving.
3 Arrange some green vegetables and the parsnips on the plates. Make a mound of potatoes and put a leg of duck on top. Pour the sauce carefully around the duck, to avoid moistening the crisp skin.

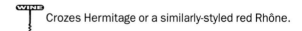 Crozes Hermitage or a similarly-styled red Rhône.

Notes
• The vegetables in the pan are called a *mirepoix*, which is discussed on page 106. A good idea with a *mirepoix* in a busy kitchen is to include onions, carrots and leeks but also any other root vegetables that badly need to be used up. They add flavour but will not be eaten, so it doesn't matter if they look a bit past their best.
• This works well with good old English farm ducks. Remember, keep the heat low for the long cooking and crispen them at a higher temperature at the end.

Fillet of Beef
with paprika potatoes, glazed shallots and *jus de* Châteauneuf du Pâpe

This is a good, straightforward recipe that could take less than half an hour to prepare but it is expensive, because of the cost of the beef. I see it as a neat and tidy dish, with the meat cut into four cylindrical shapes.

It is a dish of which the basic elements all offer opportunities for variation. For example, the glazed shallots are quick and easy but you could equally well cook them as a *confit*. Just add wine, butter and herbs and cook them in foil in the oven. The potatoes could be cooked in any number of ways, although the paprika potatoes suggested here are one of the quickest ways of cooking a potato accompaniment. And I might add a little spinach or cabbage for the beef to sit on. Whatever you choose, your vegetables should be simple and add colour (see photo on page 59). The beef itself will also have an interesting height and neatness.

Rare beef will feel very spongy and pliable when pressed gently; medium-rare will only give a little; medium gives only slightly and well done beef not at all. Whatever choice you and your guests make, let the meat rest for a while before serving. This not only helps the juices to mingle but ensures that the centre of the meat is done as you require. Medium- rare meat, for example, will not have a pink colouring all through if you serve it straight away, because the very centre will not have received the heat; there will still be a hint of bleu.

The Châteauneuf du Pâpe really helps to bring out the flavour of the sauce, which is a reduced veal *jus*.

SERVES 4

about 900g beef fillet, well trimmed, in one piece
100ml olive oil

For the paprika potatoes:
4 large baking potatoes

1 dessertspoon Hungarian paprika
30g unsalted butter
salt

For the glazed shallots:
30g unsalted butter
salt
12 shallots
100ml oil
1 dessertspoon caster sugar

For the sauce:
120ml Veal *Jus* (page 100) or beef stock
200ml Châteauneuf du Pâpe
salt and pepper

To serve:
selection of Baby Vegetables (page 177),
   e.g. carrots and mange-tout peas

To cook the beef:
1 Check the beef and remove any remaining sinew and so on. Tie it with string to achieve a neat cylindrical shape, roll it in cling film to maintain the shape and leave it to rest in the refrigerator for a few hours.
2 Preheat the oven to 200°C/400°F/Gas Mark 6. Cut the whole fillet into four neat cylindrical steaks. Dip the steaks in oil and either fry them in a hot pan or char-griddle them, to mark one side of the beef only with 'griddle marks'.
3 Seal the beef on the other sides and put it in the oven for 7-10 minutes for rare meat, 12-15 minutes for medium-rare and 15-20 minutes for medium, depending on your oven and taste. Remove from the oven and allow to rest.

For the paprika potatoes:
1 Follow the method for *Pommes Fondantes* (page 132) but cut the potatoes with a smaller cutter, about 3cm across.
2 Mix the paprika with a little water or stock and add it, with the butter, to the potato water. Cook until the potatoes are tender and remove from the remaining liquor. You need not worry about glazing the potatoes, because the colour of the paprika will be enough.

For the glazed shallots:
1 A quick way of cooking and glazing shallots: bring a saucepan of water, with the remaining butter and a little salt, to the boil; add the shallots and poach until tender. Drain and dry.
2 In a frying-pan, fry the shallots in the oil, with the sugar, until they are evenly glazed. Remove and reserve them.

For the sauce:
Reduce the veal *jus*, until it has the consistency of single cream. Add the wine and reduce again. Taste and season and pass through a fine sieve, if necessary.

To serve:
Re-heat the beef for a few minutes only, to warm it through, and remove the strings. Serve each steak with three of the paprika potatoes per portion. Garnish with some baby carrots and a few mange-tout peas. Serve the sauce over the beef.

WINE Châteauneuf du Pâpe (you can tell the real thing by the crest on the bottle).

Notes
• One idea for the potatoes would be to reduce their cooking water with a few finely-chopped shallots. The effect would be to produce a *glace* of the paprika-flavoured water and shallots, which could be spooned over the potatoes on the plate. This is quite simple and looks great; a small piece of piece of chervil would add a lovely colour to finish.

Roasted Partridge
with orange and cardamom, with creamed cabbage

This is another seasonal dish: partridge is available from November through to the end of February. Partridges can be scrawny at the beginning of the season, as they haven't fattened up for the winter. A delicious game bird, not as strong as grouse or wild duck; it's almost like chicken but with a more pronounced flavour.

The secret is to sear the birds in the pan first, to keep all the flavours and moistness in. The breasts should be served quite pink. All the elements come together well and this is a good dish to serve at Christmas time. I particularly enjoy the eastern spice (cardamom) used in a classical dish.

SERVES 4

4 whole oven-ready partridges
75ml cooking oil
4 teaspoons cardamom pods

For the sauce:
juice of 2 oranges
125ml Madeira or medium sherry
125ml Veal *Jus* (page 100)
30g unsalted butter, chilled and cubed
salt and pepper   *(continued)*

For the creamed cabbage:
1 Savoy or similar cabbage
30g unsalted butter
pinch of freshly grated nutmeg
50ml double cream
salt and white pepper

To serve:
Pommes Fondantes (page 132)

For the partridges:
1 Make twelve *Pommes Fondantes*, allowing about 30 minutes for them to cook. Preheat the oven to 220°C/425°F/Gas Mark 7.
2 Season the partridges inside and out with salt.
3 In a hot, ovenproof frying-pan, heat the oil and sear the birds on both sides, being careful not to burn or darken the skin too much. Then turn them upside-down, so that the breasts brown evenly.
4 Turn the partridges upright again and sprinkle the cardamom pods into the pan, followed by the juice of an orange and half the Madeira or sherry.
5 Cover the birds with foil and roast them in the oven for about 10 minutes.
6 Remove the birds and allow them to rest, reserving the pan and juices. De-glaze the pan by adding the rest of the Madeira or sherry and stirring; pour the mixture into a clean saucepan, with the Veal *Jus*.
7 Add the juice of the remaining orange to this pan and leave the sauce to reduce for about 8 minutes.
8 Meanwhile, carefully remove the legs from each partridge and put them back into the hot oven, to finish cooking and become crisp.
9 Carefully remove the breasts from the carcases. Break one of the carcases with a sharp, heavy knife, add this to the sauce, and cook for about 10 minutes, or until it has imparted a full, gamey flavour.

10 Pass the sauce through a fine sieve, into a clean saucepan. Whisk the cold, cubed butter into the sauce, piece by piece.
11 The partridge breasts need to be baked for about 5 minutes more, to finish them. They should be served pink. Remove the skin before serving them.

For the creamed cabbage:
1 *Chiffonade* (finely shred) the cabbage and blanch it in boiling, seasoned water. Remove and drain.
2 In a hot frying-pan, heat the butter and oil and fry the cabbage, stirring and moving it around the pan continuously, for a minute or two. Season with nutmeg, salt and pepper.
3 Add the double cream and reduce until the sauce is thick. Taste and check the seasoning.

To serve:
Make beds of the cabbage on using a straight-sided metal pastry cutter as a mould. Place the meat on the creamed cabbage. Garnish with three small fondant potatoes per person and pour the sauce carefully round.

WINE A good, oaky Rioja Gran Reserva.

Notes
• You could replace the partridge with pigeon or any other seasonal game bird. Because this is a delicate dish, it requires delicate vegetables.

Char-griddled Entrecôte of Beef
with caramelized onions and *Parisienne* potatoes

This dish is not particularly radical in its basic ingredients but is made special by the way it looks. The entrecôte is rolled (like the lamb, page 61), giving an interesting round shape when it's sliced. Char-griddling gives the beef a lovely flavour that blends so well with the sweetness of the caramelized onions. The simplicity of the sauce also complements the sweetness of the onions.

This is a winner at dinner parties, providing that you have a good, well hung piece of beef. The secret of this is to make sure, when you buy it from the butcher, that it is a rich, dark, maroon colour and not bright red. Ask your butcher for the sirloin whole, with the fat removed, and ask him to roll and tie it tightly in a cylindrical shape. Entrecôte really looks like a piece of fillet, when it's cut like this, and it is a beautiful dish to eat.

Make sure to arrange the vegetables all around the beef, so it's one integral dish.

1kg entrecôte (sirloin of beef)

For the marinade:
50ml red wine
2 garlic cloves, crushed
pinch of ground allspice
100ml olive oil
4 shallots, finely sliced
freshly grated nutmeg

For the Parisienne potatoes:
3 large potatoes
100ml cooking oil

For the caramelized onions:
1 large or two small onions, finely sliced
50g unsalted butter
100ml red wine vinegar
100ml red wine
about 100ml cheap port
100g caster sugar

For the sauce:
125ml Veal *Jus* (page 100)
50ml red wine

To serve:
selection of green vegetables (page 175), e.g. green
    beans, and Glazed Carrots

For the beef:

1 Rest the beef in the refrigerator for a couple of days before marinating to keep its cylindrical shape.

2 Mix all the marinade ingredients together in a bowl (not a metal one) big enough to take the beef in a single layer.

3 Cut the beef into four rounds 1-2cm thick. Leave them for 24 hours in the marinade, turning them occasionally if they're not evenly covered by the liquid.

4 Preheat oven to 220°C/425°F/Gas Mark 7. Char-griddle each piece of beef on both sides, to give it a charcoal flavour.

5 Remove the pieces, put them on a baking tray and roast them for 10-15 minutes, for medium meat; allow to rest for a few minutes before serving.

For the Parisienne potatoes:

1 Peel each potato and, using a *Parisienne* scoop (melon baller), cut out evenly sized balls. Poach them gently in salted water, until just tender. Drain well.

2 In a hot frying-pan, in a little oil, fry the potatoes until they are evenly browned. Remove them and put them on kitchen paper, to absorb any fat.

To caramelize the onions:

1 Heat the butter in a frying-pan and fry the onions until soft. De-glaze the pan by adding the vinegar and stirring. Add the red wine and enough port to cover; add the sugar and bring to the boil.

2 Leave to reduce until the red wine has evaporated and left the onions glazed and red.

For the sauce:

Reduce the Veal *Jus* and red wine to the consistency of single cream; season and taste the sauce.

To serve:

1 The entrecôte will have to go back into the oven for 4-5 minutes, to heat it through. Serve with some of the onions on top of each piece of beef.

2 Pour a little sauce around the beef and garnish with the potatoes and green vegetables or glazed carrots.

WINE A good St.-Emilion (Grand Cru), or a rich, deep Burgundy such as Volnay.

Notes

• You could use other cuts of beef (rump or fillet for example). The dish also works well with leg steaks of lamb.

Saddle of Venison
with juniper sauce, roasted vegetables and parsnip purée

Good venison steak doesn't need marinating and, as it's a very lean meat, it should not be cooked for very long at all. Even the slightest over-cooking makes it chewy and dry. Always serve venison rare, or medium-rare. This doesn't apply to haunch which needs a much slower cooking.

If you can get wild venison, this would be best for flavour but it is possible to get excellent farmed venison.

This is one of my favourite dishes on the menu at the Pink Geranium. Juniper berries are the perfect complementary flavour for venison but the parsnip purée is only one possible accompaniment: use celeriac or any vegetable purée.

SERVES 4

25ml cooking oil
750g saddle of venison, cut in 150g cutlets
salt and pepper

For the sauce:
150ml Veal *Jus* (page 100)
100ml red wine
4 teaspoons juniper berries
25g unsalted butter, chilled and cubed, if necessary
salt and pepper

To serve:
Rösti Potatoes (page 130)
Roasted Vegetables (page 180)
Parsnip Purée (page 176)

To cook the venison:
1 Preheat the oven to 220°C/425°F/Gas Mark 7. Pour the oil into a hot frying-pan and sear (seal) the venison steaks on all sides; season well and put the steaks in a baking dish.

2 Roast the venison for about 8 minutes, turning occasionally.
3 Remove and allow to rest and cool.
4 Prepare the Rösti Potatoes, ready for re-heating with the venison. Time your Roasted Vegetables and Parsnip Purée to be ready at the time you want to dish up.

To make the sauce:
1 Reduce the Veal *Jus* with the red wine to the consistency of single cream.
2 Add the juniper berries and cook them in the sauce for about 10 minutes, until the berries are tender.
3 Season and taste the sauce. It should have thickened naturally and become full flavoured. If it is too thick, dilute it with some water or white wine; if it's too thin, add cubes of chilled butter and whisk them quickly into the sauce.

To serve:
1 Turn the oven up to 230°C/450°F/Gas Mark 8. Put the venison and cooked rösti back in the oven together for about 5 minutes, to heat through and finish cooking.
2 Put the rösti in the centre of the plate. Slice the venison and arrange it on the rösti. Pour the sauce around and finish with the Roasted Vegetables and Parsnip Purée (see the photograph).

WINE A good, rich red Rhône Hermitage, or New World (such as an Australian Cabernet Sauvignon).

Notes
• In the photograph I have used wild venison on the bone, which I appreciate is harder to obtain. If you would like more information call my butcher (see page 60).

Guinea Fowl
with its own *confit* and wild mushroom sauce

The traditional culinary meaning of *confit* (short for confiture) is 'preserve': the implication is a cooking method designed not only to preserve the food from decay but also to conserve its moisture and flavour. With the rapid turnover of food in modern kitchens, *confit* now has a slightly different meaning. We use it to mean a method of slow cooking – such as braising – that will break down the fat and fibres in the food and enhance its flavours. It is generally used for meat and fish. There are many adaptations but we generally use the following basic recipe, which works well with most game birds as well.

Drying the mushrooms out in the oven really intensifies their flavour. People are frequently surprised and delighted by the sauce; beware, it can be a little heavy. A good tip is to use a little chicken or veal stock, to lighten the cream sauce.

SERVES 4

4 oven-ready guinea fowl
100g unsalted butter
50ml olive oil
salt and pepper

For the confit:
1kg goose fat
1 small onion, finely chopped
half a head of garlic, sliced in half horizontally
1 small leek, finely chopped
6 cloves
pinch of ground allspice
1 cinnamon stick
2 star anises
peel of 1 orange
4 bay leaves
10 fennel seeds
10 black peppercorns

For the sauce:
450g button mushrooms, thinly sliced
75ml dry Madeira or sherry
300ml double cream
450g assorted wild mushrooms, cleaned
300ml double cream
salt and pepper

To serve:
Mashed Potatoes (page 131)
double cream (optional)
olive oil (optional)
selection of vegetables, e.g. French beans (page 175),
**   Glazed Carrots (page 175) Baby Aubergines (page 177)**

To make the confit:

Preheat the oven to 150°C/300°F/Gas Mark 2-3. Cut off the legs of the guinea fowl. Put all the *confit* ingredients into the warmed goose fat in a deep baking dish and add the legs of the guinea fowl. Slowly cook on a low heat (or oven-bake) for about 2 hours, or until the meat is soft, tender and falling off the bone.

To make the sauce:

1 Turn the oven up to 220°C/425°F/Gas Mark 7. Dry the button mushrooms in the oven for about 10 minutes. This process increases the intensity of the flavours of the mushrooms and ensures that they don't make the sauce watery (mushrooms contain about 80 per cent water). Season to taste.

2 De-glaze the mushroom pan by adding the Madeira or sherry and stirring, add the juices to a deep saucepan and pour in the cream. Leave to simmer for about 30 minutes, stirring occasionally. Check the seasoning and add the wild mushrooms. Cook for a further 5 minutes and serve immediately.

To cook the guinea fowl:

1 Remove the breasts from the carcass, season, and pan sear (or griddle) in a hot pan.

2 Now roast the breasts in the hot oven for about 7-10 minutes in a little oil. Allow the breasts to rest and then carefully slice in half diagonally, at 45°.

To serve:

1 Mix the meat from the legs with the mashed potato and add a little cream and olive oil. Taste and season.

2 Put the halved breast of guinea fowl on top of the *confit* mashed potato. Give each half a quarter turn. Pour the creamy mushroom sauce over the top. Garnish with the vegetables around it.

WINE A good Médoc (Bordeaux) or Margaux.

Casserole of Braised Ox Cheek
with ginger, speck and coriander Yorkshire puddings

Ox cheek is delicious but it does take longer to braise than braising beef. It's a great dish for putting into the oven and forgetting about. An economical winter dish, we serve it at lunchtime. What I really like is larger cubes of beef, so cut your meat into fairly large pieces. The ginger flavour is prominent in the casserole but should not be overpowering.

Add coriander seeds or fresh chopped coriander to the Yorkshire puddings to bring the flavour out even more. Speck is a cured belly of pork. If you can't find it, use smoked bacon.

SERVES 4

For the beef:
2.5kg ox cheek or braising steak
100ml cooking oil
1 onion, chopped
1 carrot, chopped
1 leek, chopped
2 celery stalks, chopped
half head of garlic, sliced horizontally
4cm piece of fresh root ginger, peeled and sliced
1 dessertspoon caster sugar
sprig of fresh thyme
750ml red wine
about 1 litre Veal *Jus* (page 100)
225g speck (or smoked bacon), cut in *lardons* (batons)
salt and pepper

For the Yorkshire puddings:
Yorkshire Pudding mixture (page 146)
bunch of fresh coriander, chopped

To serve:
Roasted Vegetables (page 180)

1 Preheat the oven to 170°C/325°F/Gas Mark 3-4. Trim all the fat away from the meat and cut each ox cheek in four or five pieces.

2 Heat the oil in a large frying-pan and sear the meat until brown. Remove the meat and add the chopped vegetables (including the ginger and garlic) and caramelize in the hot pan, with the sugar.

3 Now mix the vegetables and meat together and add the thyme, red wine and enough *jus* to cover. Bring the casserole to the boil on the hob and then cook it in the oven for about 4 hours, or until the meat is very tender.

4 Meanwhile, make the Yorkshire pudding mixture, adding the chopped coriander to the batter at the end. Make the puddings large (10cm diameter) and bake them while the sauce is cooking and reducing.

5 Remove the casserole from the oven and allow the meat to cool in the liquor.

6 Remove the meat from the liquor and strain the liquor (removing and discarding the vegetables, etc.) into a clean saucepan.

7 Reduce this sauce until it's thick and rich (but not too thick).

8 Pan-fry the speck or bacon lardons in the oil. Remove with a slotted spoon, drain on kitchen paper and add them to the sauce. Taste and correct the seasoning, adding more finely chopped ginger, if necessary. Put the meat back in the sauce.

9 Serve the casserole in the Yorkshire puddings (see photo, page 147). When I use this recipe, I like to add a garnish of Roasted Vegetables (page 180) to keep it rustic looking.

WINE New World Cabernet Sauvignon (particularly Australian).

Twenty-minute Marvels

The recipes in this chapter are mostly based on ones I used on the BBC2 television programme *Ready Steady Cook*. For those of you who don't know the programme, it is a cooking competition in which two leading chefs are asked to prepare meals against the clock. The catch is that the ingredients cost less than £5, have been chosen by a member of the audience and are only shown to the chef as the clock starts ticking. Within twenty minutes, working with the member of the audience and the £5 ingredients, the chef has to create an imaginative and tasty dish. The audience decide the winner. The only extra help that I, as a competitor, receive is an amply stocked larder containing some essentials: seasonings, herbs, oils, equipment, etc. The hindrance is that the show's presenter, Fern Britton, frequently asks me to stop and explain what I am doing, so the time becomes even more tight. It's great fun, though!

The programme, which became something of a cult, is now enormously popular. It stretches one's creativity, and shows exactly what can be done with very limited budgets and even more limited time. I've won quite a few times, and also had a few disasters. The real key is adaptability. I was once presented with a Mars Bar, which I managed to convert to a toffee sauce. A bag of pulses was a big problem, and once I made some strawberry tuille (page 96) because hardly anything was in the bag! Most of all, I have been amazed at what I, and the other chefs, can actually achieve within the time. Have a look at some of the following. Most of them are my winning recipes … and I'm not saying which were my losers!

One last point I should make is that, although I took twenty minutes for these recipes, you can, of course, take longer. All I want to do is to introduce you to some good recipe ideas, and, perhaps, some new tricks and techniques to help you cook creatively and quickly.

Stir-fried Pork Fillet
with shiitake mushrooms, sake and garlic mashed potatoes

In the early days of *Ready Steady Cook*, we all used stir-fries a lot. We thought this was the only way of cooking within twenty minutes. Since then we have all progressed and wouldn't expect to win with something that unambitious, but here stir-frying is definitely the best option for the ingredients.

This is simple but very tasty. It is actually a recipe I have encouraged a group of school children to try. They particularly enjoyed the pyramid-shaped construction.

SERVES 4

350g pork fillet, cut in strips
pinch of Chinese five-spice powder
100ml oil
2 shallots, chopped
1 garlic clove, bruised and chopped
5cm piece of fresh root ginger, peeled and cut in strips
250g shiitake mushrooms
3 tablespoons sake
2 tablespoons red wine
1 tablespoon soy sauce
6 spring onions, chopped
knob of unsalted butter, chilled
splash of white wine
1 dessertspoon caster sugar
salt and pepper
6 fresh coriander leaves

To serve:
4 portions of Garlic Mashed Potatoes (page 81)
4 portions of Baby Vegetables (page 177)

1 Heat a frying-pan and season the strips of pork with salt, black pepper and five-spice powder.

2 In a little oil, sweat the shallots, garlic and ginger. Add the mushrooms and cook for 2-3 minutes.

3 Now add the pork strips and seal them all over. Cook for 5 minutes, until light brown and slightly crisp.

4 De-glaze the pan by adding the sake, red wine and soy sauce and stirring. Cook for a further 2-3 minutes; remove the pork strips before they over-cook.

5 Taste and adjust the seasoning. Reduce if necessary.

6 Sear the spring onions in a little very hot oil, add a knob of cold butter and allow it to melt; add a splash of white wine, the caster sugar and a pinch of salt and poach until softened and slightly caramelised.

7 Re-heat the strips of pork in the finished sauce and add the coriander; serve on the mash, garnished with a few simple fresh vegetables and tumble a few spring onions around as well.

WINE Southern French Grenache, or Côtes du Rhône.

Notes

• I often use rösti potatoes again here, not only because they're so quick to cook but because they're a firm favourite of mine. There are a number of potato recipes in the chapter on vegetarian dishes and vegetables. Roasted vegetables or glazed vegetables also work very well with this recipe.

• Sake can be difficult to get, unless you go to a Chinese or Japanese delicatessen. It's a dry rice wine; mirin is a sweeter version and works well. You could even use a dry wine or vermouth.

Rustic Lamb's Liver
with bacon and garlic mash, caramelized red onions and tomato sauce

I had quite a lot of letters saying how good this dish was! It really is a rustic dish and, if you like lamb's liver, it has lovely flavours. The sauce is strong; the combination of the lamb's liver stock with the tomato fondue works really well. On the show, I used canned tomatoes, which gave a good flavour, but fresh tomatoes or some of my Tomato Fondue (page 109) works very well too.

There should be no problem doing this dish in about twenty minutes. A good Sunday lunch recipe – for a change!

SERVES 4

3 or 4 large potatoes, peeled and cut in small chunks
115g unsalted butter
700g lamb's liver, with liver trimmings
150ml olive oil
leaves of a sprig of fresh rosemary, chopped
100ml cooking oil
3 red onions, sliced
4 garlic cloves, crushed to a paste
6 tomatoes, quartered
350ml dry white wine
1 dessertspoon caster sugar
60ml white wine vinegar
60ml double cream
5 or 6 rashers of lean back bacon, grilled and chopped
salt and pepper

To serve:
Roasted Vegetables (page 180)

1 Put the potatoes in a saucepan of boiling water, with seasoning and half the butter.

2 Marinate the sliced lamb's liver in the olive oil, with a little of the rosemary and seasoning.

3 In a hot pan, sweat one of the onions in a teaspoon of oil. Then add two cloves of garlic, the tomatoes and about 100ml of white wine. Cook this mixture until you have a tomato fondue (page 109).

4 Caramelize the other onions (save a couple of slices) by heating them briskly in a little oil, the sugar, vinegar and remaining wine.

5 Meanwhile, make a stock from the trimmings of the liver; sweat them in a hot saucepan with the reserved onion slices and half a clove of garlic; add a little rosemary and about 250ml of water, before leaving the stock to cook for 10 minutes.

6 When it has reduced by half, pass the stock through a fine sieve into a clean saucepan. Now process the tomato fondue mixture in the food processor and pass this through a fine sieve too. Join the two sauces together, taste and adjust the seasoning as necessary.

7 Drain the potatoes, once they are soft, and mash them. Add the remaining crushed garlic (in a paste form, to avoid lumps) and mix in well. Also add the remaining butter and the cream, until you have a smooth (but not runny), soft mash. Add the bacon and taste and season accordingly.

8 Finally, pan-fry, griddle (or even grill) the liver, until golden brown on both sides and relatively firm to the touch.

9 Serve the liver on a bed of the potato (carefully shaped in a metal ring) and pour the sauce around it. Serve with lots of caramelised onions and some roasted vegetables.

WINE A Cru Beaujolais like Juliennas or Brouilly.

Pork Rissoles

with puréed celeriac, turmeric potatoes, deep-fried leeks and garlic cream

This was quite a difficult one for me: I was handed some minced pork, which I'd never used before. Also, there was celeriac, which takes quite a bit of time to cook, and the potatoes and leeks. I didn't really know what to do at first, so I started off by making the rissoles, which I knew would hold their flavour well when coated with the breadcrumbs (simply flouring them will make them brown and tasty, too). I cut the celeriac into tiny pieces so it would cook very quickly. And I chose deep-fried leeks, which could form a tower and make the final construction look very attractive.

I know it could take twenty minutes just to read this recipe but you'll find the cooking time very quick indeed, and the result very tasty.

SERVES 4

For the rissoles:
450g minced pork
1 egg
bunch of fresh coriander, chopped
pinch of cayenne pepper or chilli powder
2 shallots or 1 onion, finely chopped
50ml cooking oil
3 tablespoons fresh breadcrumbs
plain flour
salt and pepper

For the celeriac purée:
1 celeriac, peeled and cut in small pieces
30g unsalted butter
60ml double cream
freshly grated nutmeg
salt and pepper

For the turmeric potatoes:
2 large baking potatoes
85ml chicken (or similar) stock
2 teaspoons ground turmeric
salt and pepper

For the sauce:
250ml double cream
4 garlic cloves, crushed to a paste
3 shallots, chopped
150ml dry white wine
chopped flat-leaf parsley
salt and pepper

For the deep-fried leeks:
1 large leek
plain flour, seasoned
oil, for deep-frying
salt and pepper

For the rissoles:
1 Preheat the oven to 230°C/450°F/Gas Mark 8. In a large bowl, mix the minced pork, egg, coriander, seasoning and spices.
2 Sweat the shallots in a little of the oil and then add them to the pork mixture.
3 Add about 2 tablespoons of the breadcrumbs and a little flour. Mould the mixture into rissole or burger shapes. Coat them in the remaining breadcrumbs.
4 Fry the rissoles in the remaining hot oil, until they're golden brown on both sides. Finish them in the hot oven for 5-10 minutes, until cooked through.

(continued)

For the celeriac purée:

1 Boil the celeriac in seasoned water, barely covering it, until it's soft and tender.

2 Drain and add the butter and cream and mash the celeriac with a potato masher. Season with nutmeg and salt and pepper to taste.

For the turmeric potatoes:

1 Peel and square off the potatoes and cut them in half. Using a small fluted metal pastry ring (3-4cm in diameter) cut the potatoes into 12 neat rounds. Straighten them off with a sharp knife, if necessary, so that they sit flat and straight.

2 In a large saucepan, add the stock, turmeric stock and seasoning, with 250ml water, and poach the potatoes until they are tender and have absorbed the yellow colour of the turmeric. Remove the potatoes from the water, when ready, and reserve them.

For the garlic cream sauce:

1 Boil the cream and garlic together, with the chopped shallots, for about 15 minutes, until the sauce has thickened and has taken up the flavours.

2 Now pass the sauce through a fine sieve (to remove the garlic and shallots) into a fresh saucepan. Add the white wine. Cook for 5 minutes (to remove any raw- alcohol taste) and, finally, add the chopped parsley and seasoning to taste.

For the deep-fried leeks:

Heat a minimum of 6-7cm of oil for deep-frying to 170°C (or when a cube of day-old bread browns in 30 seconds). *Chiffonade* (finely shred) the leek and toss the shreds in seasoned flour. Shake off excess flour and deep-fry in hot oil, until they start changing colour to light brown. Remove, drain and season. They will stay crisp if left for 2-3 minutes but will go soft after an hour or so.

To serve:

1 Put some celeriac purée in the centre of the plate using the cutters, with the crisp rissoles on top. Put three of the potatoes around and finally pour the garlic cream neatly around, not covering any of the food on the plate.

2 Garnish with a tower of deep-fried leeks.

WINE Southern French Languedoc or Merlot.

Notes

• Roasted vegetables also go well with this dish, although cooking more vegetables would take you longer than twenty minutes.

• You could use any mince for this dish or make a vegetarian version, using lentils or minced haricots.

Medallions of Sirloin of Beef

with cabbage, rösti potatoes and a horseradish sauce

This is a dish that I prepared during a *Ready Steady Cook* photo shoot for *TV Quick* magazine. I thought I would be asked what I wanted to cook but in fact I was given twenty minutes to create something from a set of pre-selected ingredients – just to make the photograph look realistic!

Away from the *Ready Steady Cook* kitchen I was really struggling. Most difficult was the absence of stock cubes to make a sauce; I had to use the double cream and horseradish that was in the bag. This actually reduced well and gave lots of flavour. I chose rösti potatoes, because they are actually quite quick to prepare; perhaps the fastest of the potato dishes I use.

In the end, the dish combined a number of classic flavours and textures but perhaps in a surprising blend. Ironically, despite its complex-sounding title, the dish is quite easy to prepare quickly.

This is another high, round construction, a style I enjoy and use a lot.

SERVES 2

oil, for frying
350g sirloin or rump beef, trimmed and cut in 4 even
    medallions (small rounds)
salt and pepper

For the cabbage:
1 Savoy cabbage
knob of butter
freshly grated nutmeg
salt and pepper

For the sauce:
2 shallots or 1 small onion
75ml white wine
150ml double cream
1 dessertspoon horseradish sauce
salt and pepper

To serve:
two portions of Rösti Potatoes (page 130)
1 teaspoon paprika
Deep-fried Basil Leaves (page 169)

Preheat the oven to 190°C/375°F/Gas Mark 5. Prepare the Rösti Potatoes.

To cook the beef:
1 In a hot pan, with a little oil, sear the medallions on each side (alternatively, griddle them in a char-griddle pan).
2 Remove the beef and allow it to rest. Before serving, it will need about a further 6 minutes in the oven (for medium-rare). Season well.

To cook the cabbage:
1 Finely *chiffonade* (shred) the cabbage and blanch for 2-3 minutes, in boiling, seasoned water. Then drain.
2 In a hot frying-pan, with a knob of butter, fry the cabbage, season with salt and nutmeg and serve immediately.

To make the sauce:
1 Sweat the shallots or onion in a little oil and add the white wine and reduce.
2 Add the double cream and horseradish and reduce again.
3 Taste and season; the sauce is ready when it evenly coats the back of a spoon.

To serve:
1 Place the warmed rösti in the centre of the plate and top it with a medallion of beef. Then add a spoonful of the cabbage and top again with the second beef medallion.
2 Pour the sauce around. The Deep-fried Basil Leaves can be placed on the dry parts of the plate but they will mingle with the sauce, which is fine.

 St. Emilion, or a Burgundy like Côtes de Beaune.

Notes
• As I mentioned earlier I would ideally like to serve this with some baby vegetables, or some mange-tout and carrots, scattered around the beef but not covered by the sauce.

Gâteau of Mediterranean Vegetables
with baked peppers and antiboise sauce

This was a real winner. I was presented with a load of Mediterranean vegetables, so I assumed the contestant was expecting some sort of vegetarian dish.

The construction looks impressive, but is easy. On the programme, I didn't have courgettes, but I've added them to this recipe as I feel the green of the courgettes on the top adds to the appearance. (It looks like the crab gâteau construction on page 26.)

This is not only a good vegetarian main dish in its own right but also a good vegetable dish to serve with meat. It looks as if you've gone to a lot of trouble, but in fact is probably easier than trying to serve several different vegetables separately.

SERVES 4

3 courgettes, sliced thinly on a mandolin (see page 90)
150ml cooking oil
2 aubergines, sliced 5mm thick
1 red pepper
1 yellow pepper
12 beef or plum tomatoes, sliced
mozzarella cheese
leaves of a generous sprig of fresh basil, *chiffonaded* **(finely shredded)**
salt and pepper

To serve:
250ml Antiboise Sauce (page 104)

1 Preheat the oven to 230°C/450°F/Gas Mark 8. Bring some water and salt to the boil in a saucepan, in order to blanch the courgettes. Blanch the thinly sliced courgettes in the seasoned water for 30 seconds. Refresh in iced water.

2 Heat a frying-pan with a little of the oil until smoking. Fry (or griddle) the sliced aubergine until it's golden brown on both sides and drain each slice on kitchen paper.

3 In a very hot frying-pan (or char-griddle, to give the criss-cross effect shown in the photograph), sear the peppers (with a little more oil) until they're dark all over. Bake in the oven for about 20 minutes. Then remove to a clean container and cover with cling film, so the trapped steam helps the outer skin to lift, making peeling easier.

4 Turn the oven down to 200°C/400°F/Gas Mark 6. Using a plain metal pastry ring as a mould, put a slice of aubergine in the ring, followed by a slice of tomato and some mozzarella cheese, followed by a little basil *chiffonade* and some sliced courgettes. Season each layer.

5 Repeat the process twice more, until you end up with a slice of aubergine on top. Now finish the dish with slices of the courgette. Bake for 10 minutes. Serve the warm sauce around it, with slices of the baked pepper.

WINE A gutsy southern Italian Salice Salentino.

Notes
• These vegetable gâteaux can be prepared well in advance, even the day before. You simply baste them with a little melted butter and cover them with foil, which seals the food and prevents it from discolouring. When ready, pop them into the oven for about 10 minutes before serving; the butter melts and poaches the vegetables.
• Sauces can be varied in this recipe. Perhaps a *Beurre Blanc* (page 110) or Tomato Fondue (page 109). Also, you could add other ingredients to the vegetable layers.

Baked Fillet of Cod
with a herb crust, Mediterranean vegetables and tomato fondue

Mediterranean flavours work well with fish. Cod is relatively inexpensive and a herb crust is easy to make and gives cod a dynamic flavour and colour. This dish is great with roasted peppers as well. The fish cooks very quickly, so be careful; don't wait for the crust to go dark brown or the fish will be over-cooked. This is a matter of timing; if you are unsure, serve a moment too soon rather than too late. This dish needs to be cooked and served straight away; this is not a recipe for which much can be done in advance.

SERVES 2

350g fresh cod fillet
Herb Crust (page 168)
1 courgette
oil, for frying
1 small aubergine, sliced 1cm thick
Tomato Fondue (page 109)
125ml white wine
salt and pepper
1 tablespoon coriander leaves, chopped

1 Preheat the oven to 190°C/375°F/Gas Mark 5. Trim and neatly bone the cod fillet, to produce an evenly shaped piece of fish. Season and coat with the Herb Crust.
2 Slice the courgette thinly, lengthways, to produce thin elongated strips. Fry in a hot pan or on a char-griddle pan, until just tender.
3 Season the aubergine slices and fry them in hot oil until golden brown on each side.
4 Prepare the Tomato Fondue.
5 Place the fish on a piece of baking parchment and pour a little wine around it. Bake for 8-10 minutes.
6 Lay the vegetables on the plate and place the cod on top. Pour the Tomato Fondue around and finish with some fresh coriander leaves.

WINE A lightish Sauvignon Blanc, such as a French Country Wine, or Sancerre.

Notes
• This dish also works brilliantly using salmon.

Rosemary-roasted Monkfish
with leeks and wild mushrooms and Niçoise *beurre blanc*

I used this in a *Ready Steady Cook* demonstration at the Pink Geranium for a fund-raising event. This is a very good dish, with a lot of Mediterranean flavours. It's very colourful too and easy to create. It won, but I was the only competitor!

I recommend marinating the monkfish for an hour to help intensify the flavours, but if you're short of time, you won't be able to do this. Don't worry.

SERVES 4

900g monkfish tails (about 4 tails), on the bone
100ml olive oil, plus extra, for frying
leaves of a sprig of fresh rosemary, chopped
100g plain flour, seasoned
salt and pepper

For the mushrooms and leeks:
225g wild mushrooms, cleaned
oil, for frying
12 baby leeks, chopped
60g unsalted butter
100 ml dry white wine
salt and pepper

For the sauce:
Beurre Blanc (page 110)
60g stoned black olives
60g Tomato Concassé (page 25)
squeeze of lemon juice
60g fresh chives, finely chopped
salt and pepper

To serve:
about 40 French beans

To cook the monkfish:
1 Preheat the oven to 200°C/400°F/Gas Mark 6. The monkfish tails, of about 250g each, should be marinated for about 1 hour in the olive oil, with the rosemary.
2 When marinated, dry the fish and coat the tails with seasoned flour, tapping off any excess.
3 In a little olive oil, in a very hot pan, fry and seal the monkfish on both sides, until golden. Remove and bake for about 10 minutes.
4 Remove from the oven and allow to rest.

To cook the mushrooms and leeks:
1 Sweat the mushrooms in a hot frying-pan, with a little oil. Add the prepared baby leeks, butter and a splash of white wine.
2 Cook until the liquid almost dries. Taste and season.

For the sauce:
1 Follow the recipe for *Beurre Blanc* and, once the sauce has been passed into a clean saucepan, add the olives and Tomato *Concassé*. Warm them gently and carefully, to prevent the sauce from separating.
2 Check the seasoning and adjust it, if necessary; add a squeeze from half a lemon and, finally, the chopped chives.

To serve:
1 Drop the green beans into boiling, seasoned water; cook until *al dente*. Put a bed of leeks and mushrooms on serving plates and put a monkfish tail on top of each. Pour the sauce around the fish. Sprinkle the beans around and serve.

WINE A light Chardonnay like a Chablis, or a greenish-white Italian, such as Pinot Grigio.

Notes
• This recipe would also work well with Mashed Potatoes (page 131) or home-made chips. If you are doing chips, cut them relatively thick. Blanch them briefly and drain them before dipping them into hot fat. Let the chips fry until golden brown, remove from the fat, dry on kitchen paper and lightly season before serving. Wonderful.
• Either serve the chips separately or criss-cross them around the monkfish on the same plate.

Galette of Barbary Duck Breast
with lentils, juniper sauce and roasted vegetables

This is quite complex for twenty minutes; I must have added a few things since using this particular recipe on the programme. However, it can still be done very quickly indeed and it proves that some extremely ambitious-sounding recipes can be created with little effort and time. This is a good way of making a single duck breast go further, too. It's a good treatment for plump, tender Barbary duck breasts, which benefit from being served while still slightly pink in the middle, in contrast to the slow-cooked recipe for crispy duck on page 66.

SERVES 2

For the galettes:
1 large baking potato, peeled
100ml light olive oil
salt and pepper

For the duck breasts:
25g unsalted butter
1 dessertspoon clear honey
1 teaspoon paprika
2 barbary duck breasts
salt and pepper

For the lentils:
100g Puy lentils or 200g canned lentils
125ml Chicken Stock (page 103) or stock cube
1 small onion and 1 celery stick, finely chopped, and 1 fresh thyme sprig (optional)
salt and pepper

For the roasted vegetables:
1 large carrot
2 celery sticks
1 leek
salt and pepper; sugar

For the sauce:
125ml dark Chicken Stock, or a chicken stock cube
125ml red wine
50g juniper berries
100g light brown sugar
15ml gin (optional)
salt and pepper

To make the galettes:
1 Slice the potatoes thinly, using a mandolin if you have one (see photos).

2 In a hot frying-pan with a little of the oil, overlap three or four slices to form a circle and fry until golden brown. Turn over and cook the other side. Drain on kitchen paper. Season. Repeat to make four neat galettes.

(continued)

To cook the duck breasts:

1 Preheat the oven to 230°C/450°F/Gas Mark 8. Make a simple glaze to enhance the flavour and the crispness of the skin, by melting the butter with the honey and paprika. Mix well over a medium heat and allow to cool a little before use.

2 Cover the skins of the duck breasts with the glaze.

3 In a little oil in a hot pan, fry the duck breasts skin-down, so that the glaze crispens the skin and flavours the duck.

4 Put the duck breasts on a baking tray and roast for about 15 minutes; they should still be pink. Allow to rest for a couple of minutes before slicing and serving.

To cook the lentils:

Whilst the duck is cooking, bring the lentils to the boil in the light stock (with the onion, celery and thyme, if using). Puy lentils cook quickly, in about 20 minutes; canned lentils will heat through in minutes. Drain when still slightly *al dente*.

To roast the vegetables:

1 Turn the oven down to 190°C/375°F/Gas Mark 5. Cut the carrot, celery and leek into lozenge shapes about 5cm long (see photo).

2 In a very hot ovenproof frying-pan, with a little oil, fry the carrots until they are brown. Season with a little sugar and salt. The sugar will glaze and caramelize the carrots.

3 Once the carrots have coloured, add the leeks and then the celery to the pan and season again with some more salt and sugar.

4 When glazed, put the pan into the oven and roast the vegetables until cooked and tender.

To make the sauce:

1 Reduce the stock by half, with the wine, and add the juniper berries.

2 Reduce again until light but slightly syrupy. Add the gin (if using) and bring back to the boil.

3 Pass through a sieve before serving.

To serve:

1 Place one potato galette on each plate, spread lentils on this and top with the slices of duck breast.

2 Pour some sauce over the top and place another galette on top.

3 Garnish with the roasted vegetables, crossed over each other, and serve.

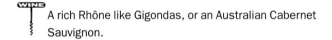

WINE A rich Rhône like Gigondas, or an Australian Cabernet Sauvignon.

Notes

• I would certainly serve more potatoes separately, say *Pommes Fondantes* or a good mash (page 132), with this recipe.

• The layers of lentils could be replaced with spinach, which would also work very well.

Marinated Chump of Lamb
with rosemary and garlic and mushroom risotto

The version of this I cooked on *Ready Steady Cook* was more complicated than this, because I prepared two sauces and some garlic confit as well (see page 170). I was probably being a bit flash!

Chump of lamb is the rump cut; although it has more fat on it than the loin, it has better flavour and responds well to being marinated, even if only for a short time. Char-griddling gives excellent Mediterranean-style flavours to this rustic dish, which eats beautifully when cooked medium or rare. It works well accompanied by *Dauphinoise* Potatoes (page 132), if you're not using risotto.

SERVES 4

300g risotto (use recipe on page 128, omitting spinach and Stilton)
4 chumps lamb, cut in half to make 8 pieces
1 large sprig fresh rosemary
3 garlic cloves, peeled and sliced
olive oil
seasoning
fresh basil, finely shredded

either
1 vegetable stock cube
1 small teaspoon yeast extract (Marmite)
dash red wine

or
250ml vegetable stock (see page 102) or a meat stock

1 Place the lamb in a pan or dish with the rosemary and garlic, season with salt and pepper and add enough olive oil to cover the lamb.
2 Cover the pan or dish and let stand for at least five minutes. If you are able to plan ahead, leave it for a few hours.
3 Get your char-griddle or frying pan smoking hot. Lift each chump out of the marinade, and griddle to seal on all sides.
4 Remove immediately and roast in a hot oven for about 10 minutes. After removing, allow to rest for a few more minutes. In the meantime, make up the risotto.
5 With a short space of time, I'd recommend making up a vegetable stock cube to 250ml of liquid, whisking in the yeast extract and wine for a quick, flavoursome stock (alternatively defrost frozen cubes of home-made stock).
6 Reduce the stock a little over a medium heat, seasoning to taste. Add chiffonaded basil just before pouring around lamb.

Notes
• To serve, I'd suggest moulding the risotto in a large straight-sided metal pastry cutter placed in the centre of the plate. Remove the metal ring, and arrange the lamb, thinly sliced, on top. Pour a little *jus* around, garnished with roasted carrots and leeks if you have time to make these.
• Even if you can only marinate the lamb for a few minutes, save the marinade for later uses.

Hot Banana or Strawberry Soufflé

You can imagine my reaction when I was handed a bag of bananas and other fruit... and nothing else. Fruit salad didn't seem very exciting and would certainly not have won. 'Soufflé' went through my mind, but soufflés usually take twenty minutes in the oven alone, and I still had to make it. But once I'd started, I couldn't turn back – there were five million people watching!

Banana blends well and easily into the soufflé. You can also use any liqueur and it can be served with many different sauces; *crème de banane* is especially nice. On the show, I served it with caramelized fruit. I peeled some of the fruit; with others, like apples, I left the skin on. I then dusted it with lots of icing sugar and put it under the grill to crisp and glaze, like a *crème brûlée* topping. Then I served the fruit around it.

I recall that the grill I had only came on when the door was open; this was a safety device. I asked the contestant to put the fruit under the grill, which she did, and shut the door. It was only with a few minutes left that we realised the fruit wasn't cooking very well; in fact, it wasn't cooking at all!

SERVES 2

40g unsalted butter
40g plain flour
250ml milk
4 eggs, separated
60g sugar
1 ripe banana
dash of *crème de banane* liqueur (optional)

To serve:
Butterscotch Sauce (page 121), Caramel Sauce (page 119) or *Crème Anglaise* (page 120)

1 Preheat the oven to 200°C/400°F/Gas Mark 6 and butter and sugar two ramekin dishes. Make the soufflé base: melt the butter in a saucepan, sift in the flour and blend the mixture to a *roux*. Cook the *roux* a little, gradually add the milk and whisk it in and then bring the sauce to the boil.
2 Whisk the egg yolks and sugar together until they are pale coloured. Fold this mixture into the soufflé base. Then, with a wooden spoon, stir well and cook for about 5 minutes.
3 Whisk the egg whites until they stand in peaks.
4 Mash the banana. Mix the soufflé base into the banana (add the liqueur now, if you are using it).
5 Fold in the egg whites; pour mixture into ramekin dishes.
6 Bake in the centre of the oven until risen and golden brown, approximately 15 minutes. Dust with icing sugar and serve immediately, with Butterscotch or Caramel Sauce or *Crème Anglaise*.

WINE Late-harvest Australian Botrytis Sèmillon.

Notes
• The secret of a good soufflé is in the buttering of the ramekin, so that the soufflé doesn't stick to the sides or the lip and comes up straight. If you have plenty of time, buttering the ramekins, putting them into the refrigerator for a while and then buttering them again before dusting them with caster sugar is the best way. I didn't have time!
• Make a strawberry soufflé in the same way. Hull and chop 250g strawberries and divide half between the ramekins. Make the rest into a *Coulis* (see page 122). Mix 2 dessert-spoons of *Coulis* into the soufflé base and make the soufflé in the same way. Serve with the remaining *Coulis*. This is my favourite soufflé for the summer (see photo).

Brandy Snaps

Brandy snaps are quick and easy, and here is a straightforward recipe for them. Mould the mixture into whatever shape you prefer: rolls are good, but so are basket shapes filled with ice cream, fruit or even a cold mousse.

135g unsalted butter
40g sugar
120g plain flour
120g golden syrup
pinch of ground ginger

1 Preheat the oven to 200°C/400°F/Gas Mark 6. Blend all the ingredients together. Mould the mixture into marble-sized balls, in your hands.
2 Place the balls on a baking tray lined with baking parchment, about 8cm apart. Press down on each, to make small discs.
3 Bake until the discs have spread out thinly and turned brown evenly.
4 Remove the tray from the oven and allow to cool for 2-3 minutes. Carefully remove the cooked biscuits with a palette knife and mould them around a ramekin, dariole mould or shape of your choice, while they are still warm and flexible, to produce a neat brandy snap basket shape. Alternatively, wrap them round the handle of a wooden spoon, to produce roll shapes.

Notes
• Brandy snap baskets will mould neatly inside a ramekin dish or dariole mould. They firm up pretty quickly as they cool, however, so you'll need to work speedily. A trio of ice creams or sorbets (three small scoops, each of a different flavour) in a brandy snap basket is a very simple and very effective dessert. Or try *Crème Chantilly* (page 119). Mini-baskets are also excellent for *petits fours*.
• Alternatively, leave the discs to set flat on a baking tray, then build up a *mille feuille* dessert with a layer of brandy snap and a circle of piped White or Dark Chocolate Mousse (pages 156-157). Repeat this using three discs per portion, finishing with a disc on top, dusted liberally with icing sugar. Serve this with a *coulis* (page 122), or an orange-flavoured Anglaise Sauce (page 120).

Tuille Pastry

I remember once on *Ready Steady Cook* being handed a bag with just some strawberries, icing sugar and flour. Tuille pastry was my only hope. All you do is mix the ingredients together and, once you have your paste, add the crushed almonds and lemon or lime zest.

Once it has been in the oven, the tuille mixture can be moulded into basket shapes on an upturned tea cup or dariole mould; these can be filled with ice cream and fruit. Alternatively, the mix can be left flat and used in a *mille feuille*, maybe filled with a chocolate mousse, stacked high and dusted with icing sugar. You can also try arranging flakes of almond neatly around the discs of pastry, which you have spread on baking trays. When they are cooked, the almonds will stand up slightly from the pastry.

It's a very versatile pastry, which can be used in lots of different ways for quick desserts.

60g caster sugar
35g soft or plain flour
1 egg
15g softened butter
1 vanilla pod
zest of 1 lemon or lime
nibbed almonds, toasted (or flakes, chopped and toasted)

1 Preheat the oven to 220°C/425°F/Gas Mark 8. Whisk the sugar into the egg, until it is dissolved and the mixture is pale in colour.
2 Sift in the flour.
3 Whisk in the butter. Split open the vanilla pod with a sharp knife and scrape the seeds of the vanilla into the bowl.
4 Add the zest of lemon or lime and the crushed almonds. The paste should now be quite thick, but spreadable.
5 Using a plastic ring, cut out of a plastic lid or container about 7cm in diameter as a template. Leave at least a 1cm gap around the circles of tuille, to allow room during cooking.
8 Bake for about 5 minutes, or until brown.
9 Remove the pastry discs whilst warm and mould them inside a round-bottomed coffee cup or ramekin, to form a basket shape, as you would for brandy snaps.

Notes

• When you soften the butter, don't let it get runny; I call the ideal consistency 'custard butter'.
• Tuilles can be used in the same way as brandy snaps (see page 96), and are also excellent as *petits fours* with coffee. Both of these quick dessert basics always have very impressive results.

Blackberry Soufflé Pancakes
with cinnamon ice cream

If you have ice cream already made, this is a definite twenty-minute standby. The pancake filling, more a light mousse than a proper soufflé, crisps in the oven with the help of the sugar, and serving it with warmed blackberries (try other fruits, too) brings all the contrasting flavours and textures alive. It's also very exciting seeing the pancakes rise!

SERVES 4

4 pancakes (see page 150)
300g fresh (or frozen) blackberries
75g caster sugar
100ml cold water
6 egg whites
cinnamon ice cream (see page 166; follow basic recipe and
    add cinnamon to taste)

1 Make up the pancakes (you can also do this in advance).
2 Make a blackberry *coulis* by blending half the berries in a food processor with a mixture of 25g caster sugar and 100ml water. (If you look at the *Coulis* recipe on page 122, this consititues the stock syrup.)
3 Pass through a fine sieve into a clean bowl.

4 Whisk the egg whites until semi-stiff; add 25g caster sugar and whisk for just 10 seconds more.
5 Fold in half of the blackberry *coulis*.
6 Line a metal tray with baking greased parchment or greaseproof paper, and lay out the pancakes. Spoon a portion of the egg and blackberry mixture on to one half of each pancake and fold the other side over. Sprinkle the remaining sugar over the pancakes, and bake in the middle of a preheated oven until risen at 200°C/400°F/Gas Mark 6, usually 10 minutes. Avoid opening the door for the first 5 minutes.
7 Meanwhile warm the remaining *coulis* with the remaining whole berries; when the pancakes are ready, serve this sauce to the side with the ice cream.

Notes

• After you've made this a few times, you can try a more ambitious method of presentation by building a tower of three. Trim the pancakes smaller by cutting around the edge of a side plate laid over the top; place the egg and berry mixture in the centre of the first one, lay over the second pancake, repeat, and finish with a third pancake, sprinkling with sugar.

Stocks and Sauces

The quality of a sauce is as important to the dish as the meat or fish. A poor sauce will ruin good food. If you are unsure about a sauce as you are about to serve, ignore it! Plain food is better than a poor sauce. I don't want to sound too disapproving here, but I have had excellent Dover sole spoiled by thick, floury sauces. The flavour of the same fish, however, could be enhanced by the addition of a well cooked *velouté*.

Stocks are very important, as they frequently form the base of other recipes, particularly sauces. Stocks, therefore, have recipes. They are not dustbins for any old things you have knocking around in the kitchen. Of course, you can vary recipes slightly, by using sensible substitutes, but you can also lose flavours altogether if you try to make drastic changes. It is as important to stick to a stock recipe as it is a method for cooking lobster.

Having run the risk of putting you off making your own stocks, I can only stress just how great they are. A good New Year's resolution would be to throw away all your stock cubes. Then have a stock day and freeze the home-made stocks in ice-cube trays, to use the cubes later one at a time. Once you have frozen the stock cubes, transfer them to freezer bags. But, remember to be scrupulous about hygiene when making stocks. Cool them as quickly as possible and get them into the refrigerator as soon as you can. If you hold them overnight, for example, to allow the fat to separate, boil them up again before cooling and freezing. Use frozen stock within a couple of months, for the best results.

Also in this chapter are a selection of dressings and marinades, as well as some recipes for sweet sauces (see Puddings, page 151). Again, try to stick to the ingredients, and ensure you allow plenty of time for

Veal *Jus*

Where would we be without veal *jus*? Yes, lamb *jus* is good – for lamb dishes only – but veal *jus* will do for every other type of meat. It is the basis of just about all the sauces that come out of any commercial kitchen. For me, it's vital to have some available, all the time.

Veal bones are ideal as the basis for this sauce, because they have quite a simple flavour. They have a full, but not complex, taste. In a small kitchen, where there is no space to store stocks for every meat, this is the stock to have in supply and then supplement for other dishes. We often use flavours from game, such as venison or pigeon, or add Madeira, red wine, *cassis*, whisky: it is so adaptable.

I have even used veal *jus* with a Fish *Velouté* Sauce (page 107). It comes out a rather strange colour but is full of flavour and makes a perfect red wine sauce for fish.

Make plenty at one go, and throw away your stock cubes. It is fairly time-consuming, with two stages of straining, and you'll need to pester your butcher to get the veal bones. Make it a day or two before for the first time you use it and store the rest. Saving it for a day or two before using it first will allow any remaining fats in the sauce to rise to the top, so you can scrape it off.

You will also note that this sauce has no flour or other thickening agent. It is a pure sauce, thickened naturally. It is very special and well worth the trouble. No chef would be without it.

12kg may seem like a lot of veal bones, but they are heavy, so the quantity may not be as large as it seems. If you don't have a large enough pan, simply halve the recipe.

MAKES ABOUT 4 LITRES

12kg veal bones
1 jar of honey (about 125g)
5 carrots
2 onions
1 head of celery
1 leek
1 head of garlic
1 bay leaf
peppercorns
500g can tomatoes
1 tablespoon tomato purée
1 calf's foot, halved, or 3 or 4 gelatine leaves
2 litres red wine
salt and pepper

1 Preheat the oven to 230°C/450°F/Gas Mark 8. Cut the veal bones into small and manageable pieces (or ask your butcher to do this). Roast them in a large baking tray, with the honey poured over, until golden brown (usually takes about an hour).

2 Tip the roasted bones into a large saucepan and add all the vegetables, peeled but left whole. Also add the bay leaf, peppercorns, tomatoes, tomato purée and calf's foot.

3 Fill the saucepan with cold water, just to cover the bones and bring to the boil.

4 Once boiling, skim the surface, removing the fat. Leave the stock to simmer for approximately 10 hours, until it has reduced by about two-thirds.

5 At this stage, the stock is ready to be passed through a medium-size *chinois* (conical) sieve into a clean saucepan, removing the bones, vegetables, etc.

6 Add the red wine, bring to the boil and reduce by about half. This will take about an hour.

7 Now pass again through a sieve lined with wet muslin. This will ensure that no impurities stay in the juice.

8 Reserve in clean plastic containers and keep in the refrigerator. Season when you add it to your recipe.

Notes

• I always use vegetables whole in this recipe; if you cut them up, they turn into a mush in the stock and make the sauce cloudy and over-flavoured. Another tip is to roast the bones until *well* browned, which gives good colour and depth of flavour. The calf's foot helps to thicken it with natural gelatine; if you can't get a calf's foot, use three or four leaves of gelatine to 450ml of stock.

Court Bouillon

This is ideal for poaching fish, shellfish and salmon. Cooked in *court bouillon*, with its herbs and lemon, all types of fish pick up a wonderful flavour. It is a little like a fish stock, but made without bones.

Court bouillon is particularly good for cooking whole salmon, which can occasionally be a little earthy or lacking in taste.

MAKES ABOUT 3 LITRES

5 leeks, chopped
2 carrots, chopped
2 celery sticks, chopped
6 shallots, chopped
2 onions, chopped
1 fennel bulb, chopped
1 head of garlic, halved horizontally
fresh thyme sprig
fresh parsley sprig
12 white peppercorns
grated zest and juice of 2 lemons
350ml dry white wine
about 15g salt

1 Put all the vegetables and herbs in a large pan, cover with cold water and bring to the boil.

2 Add the peppercorns, lemon zest, juice and wine and simmer for about 30 minutes.

3 Pass through muslin or a fine sieve and store until you are ready to use it.

Notes

• *Court bouillon* will freeze but is only at its best for a maximum of 2 months.

Vegetable Stock

This is a very easy to make, light stock. It will go well with a range of vegetable and meat dishes.

As with the other stocks in this chapter, please remember that the recipe works as it is. If you substitute different ingredients, do so with care. Always try to swap like for like, and also stick to the correct quantities.

MAKES ABOUT 500ML

1 onion or 2 shallots, finely chopped
1 garlic clove, finely chopped
half a bulb of fennel, sliced
1 medium leek, finely chopped
30g white mushroom trimmings, finely chopped
25g unsalted butter
25ml vegetable cooking oil
2 fresh tarragon sprigs, finely chopped
2 fresh coriander sprigs, finely chopped

1 With the exception of the chopped herbs, put all the ingredients in a large saucepan. Sweat off for 2-3 minutes, without letting the vegetables colour.
2 Add 500ml of water, bring to the boil and leave to simmer slowly for no more than 15 minutes.
3 Add the chopped herbs and cook for 5 more minutes.
4 Sieve (through muslin for a very fine stock, using the back of a ladle to force through the flavours) to remove the bits and pieces.
5 Use immediately or store in a plastic container until required. Vegetable stock can be frozen.

Notes
• Try not to let the cooking time of this recipe exceed 20 minutes, as you will then start to lose the freshness and aromas of the vegetables and herbs.
• Don't season this stock during the cooking process, only adding white pepper and a little salt to taste when you finally serve it.
• This is ideal for making soups or vegetarian sauces by reducing the finished stock and adding double cream or even yoghurt to finish, finally adding fresh soft green herbs. As it freezes so well, make plenty up in advance.

Chicken Stock

This is made in much the same way as any stock. With roasted bones, the flavour is quite strong and the colour is slightly darker. For a lighter in colour, creamy sauce, boil the bones. I do recommend the former however; in my opinion, the darker colour is more appealing. This is a very good basic sauce stock.

MAKES 1 LITRE

1kg chicken carcases, broken up and roasted until golden
100g mushrooms, finely chopped
100g carrots, finely chopped
1 shallot, finely chopped
1 leek
1 small celery stick
1 garlic clove, crushed
100ml dry white wine
2 litres cold water
1 bouquet garni
1 small white onion
1 clove

1 Put the roasted bones into a saucepan, with the vegetables.

2 Bring to the boil, add the wine and leave to simmer, until the liquid has almost completely evaporated.

3 Add the cold water, bouquet garni, onion and clove. Bring to the boil.

4 Simmer slowly over a low heat for 3 hours, skimming the surface occasionally.

5 Pass the stock through a fine sieve and leave it to cool. Remove any fat from the surface and keep it in the refrigerator, until needed.

Notes

• If you are going to use it immediately, I suggest reducing this stock a little more, after straining it. It's best to line the sieve with muslin, which removes even more particles, leaving a clearer, cleaner-tasting stock.

• If you are freezing it, remember to reduce it a little after thawing. This stock freezes very well, for up to six months. Only use it for chicken or other fowl dishes.

Antiboise Sauce

This is a powerful, oil-based sauce which adds the wonderful flavours of fresh garlic and shallots to a dish. I'm not sure where the name comes from. We use this sauce a lot in the kitchen at the Pink Geranium; it's very versatile. Because it's so simple, it keeps well (for months, if you give it the chance).

SERVES ABOUT 4

2 shallots, finely and neatly chopped
1 garlic clove, crushed to a paste
150ml extra virgin olive oil
juice of 1 lemon or lime
finely chopped fresh coriander
salt and pepper

1 Sweat the shallots and garlic in some of the oil in a thick-bottomed pan. Do not allow to colour. Add the rest of the oil and leave to simmer for about 15 minutes, until the shallots are soft and tender.

2 Allow the sauce to rest, so the flavours infuse the oil.

3 Add the lemon juice and seasoning to taste. Keep in an airtight container until you want to use it.

4 When needed, re-heat and taste, season again, if necessary, add the coriander and serve at once.

Notes

• You could add a little Tomato *Concassé* (page 25), for colour, at stage 4, or various other herbs. I sometimes add baked pepper or sun-dried pimento slices too.

Savoury *Sabayon* Sauce

SERVES 4-6

3 egg yolks
2 tablespoons warm water
juice of 1 lemon
pinch of salt
120ml champagne or white wine, warmed
chopped fresh chives
salt and pepper

1 Whisk the yolks in a round-bottomed, stainless steel bowl until they are pale in colour. Add the warm water (which will help to stabilize the sauce at this stage).

2 Over a saucepan of boiling water, keep whisking the yolks and now add the lemon juice and salt and the warmed champagne or wine.

3 Whisk until the mixture has doubled in size. Season and taste and add the chives.

4 Neatly and carefully coat the base of each plate with a little *sabayon* and then glaze the sauce under a hot grill or with a blow torch, until it has light brown streaks. Serve your meat, fish, or whatever on top of the sauce.

Notes

• A sweet *sabayon* sauce can be made in the same way. Omit the lemon juice and salt and add 60g caster sugar to the eggs; increase the champagne (or you can use white wine; it wouldn't have to be sweet) to about 200ml.

Lobster Sauce

This sauce is made from shells of lobster or prawns. Never throw any of them away; they are full of flavour. Wrap them in cling film and keep them in the freezer until you're ready to make stock from them. What we do here is roast the shells to intensify the flavour. When sieving the sauce, be sure to press hard (bang the shells a little) as this will release even more flavour. By this stage, the shells will be soft, so tiny fragments will not flake off into the stock.

Remember that this is a strongly flavoured sauce, used frequently as a base for others. One important tip is not to overdo the cream; it should be thick, but not too creamy.

MAKES ABOUT 500ML

450g lobster or prawn shells
3 garlic cloves
100g *mirepoix* (see Notes)
4 tomatoes
125ml brandy
250ml water or fish stock (enough to cover a lobster)
150ml double cream
100ml white wine, if necessary
50g unsalted butter, chilled and cubed
small fresh dill sprig, chopped
small fresh tarragon sprig, chopped
salt and pepper

1 Preheat the oven to 230°C/450°F/Gas Mark 8. Bake the shells until they're brown, with the garlic and vegetables.
2 To bring together all the flavours, including those from the bottom of the roasting tin, de-glaze the tin by pouring in the brandy and stirring with a wooden spoon, removing any juices that have stuck to the pan. Put the shells with these juices into a deep saucepan. Add the tomatoes, vegetables and water or stock and bring to the boil.
3 Skim and leave to simmer for 40 minutes, until reduced by about half.
4 Add the cream and reduce well.
5 Taste and season and then strain the liquid through a metal sieve, into a clean saucepan, pressing down on the lobster shells with a spoon or ladle, to extract all the flavours.
6 Reduce again and adjust the seasoning.
7 Finally, add some wine, if necessary, to thin the sauce. Add the cubes of butter and whisk them in until they melt. Add the chopped herbs before serving.

Notes
• A *mirepoix* is a mixture of roughly chopped vegetables and meat, used to enhance the flavour of sauces. For lobster sauce, I use a *mirepoix* consisting of such vegetables as celery, onion, mushrooms, leeks and a fennel bulb. The vegetables should be cooked with the lobster shells in a little water for added flavour. Fish stock will add even more flavour than water; use it if you have some handy, but I wouldn't bother making it especially.
• This sauce also makes a superb lobster bisque, even nicer with pieces of fresh lobster in it. It freezes well (I advise making up lots and freezing) and can be used for many sauces, soups and so on.

Fish *Velouté* Sauce

This fish *velouté* is a fish stock with added cream, but don't use this as a stock recipe without the cream. The reason for this is that cooking the bones for as long as I suggest here will start to turn the stock cloudy. With cream, of course, this doesn't matter, but a stock should be clear. Cooking for the 45 minutes does ensure that you get maximum flavour from the bones and vegetables.

Fish *velouté* is a base sauce, which, once made, can be developed into a multitude of others. The stored sauce can be thinned down with a little white wine or vermouth. I highly recommend it with any fish dish.

SERVES 8

1 onion, roughly chopped
1 leek, roughly chopped
half a celery head, roughly chopped
75g mushroom trimmings, stalks, etc.
2 garlic cloves, crushed
1 small fennel bulb, roughly chopped
100g cooking oil, or unsalted butter
500g fish bones, chopped into small pieces
250ml dry white wine
250ml double cream
salt and pepper

1 Sauté the vegetables in the oil or butter, until tender.
2 Add the fish bones and stir well.
3 De-glaze to bring together the flavours by adding the wine to the pan, and stir well.
4 Cover the bones with cold water and bring to the boil. Skim the surface and set pan on a fast simmer; simmer for about 45 minutes, or until nearly reduced by half.
5 Pass the stock through a muslin-lined sieve into a clean pan and reduce it again by about half.
6 Add the double cream and reduce again to thicken the sauce. When it is of a coating consistency, check the flavour, season and reserve until needed.

Notes

• Adding a little white wine when you re-use the sauce will add slightly to the flavour. Dry white wines and vermouth are particularly good. You could also consider a few fresh herbs or some lemon or lime juice.

Barbecue Sauce

I vary this recipe, depending on how I feel. I might add more orange juice and reduce the amount of meat stock, reduce the tomato ketchup and add some vinegar, or use tomato purée. The sweet-and-sour nature is what changes most. The principal ingredients are the right ones for a good barbecue sauce. It's one of those stand-bys that you can have in the freezer for an informal dinner or lunch party. It is not really special enough for a dinner party sauce. It's great with your sausages and char-griddled chicken breasts; you would not choose to use it, however, with your fillets of beef!

SERVES 6

150ml Veal *Jus* (page 100) or stock cube if you have no
   alternative
150ml red wine
150ml orange juice
2 shallots, finely chopped
2 garlic cloves, finely chopped
2 dessertspoons tomato ketchup
flesh of 3 beef tomatoes, puréed or 100ml Tomato Fondue
   (page 109)
1 dessertspoon white wine vinegar
1 dessertspoon honey
3 dessertspoons soy sauce
salt and pepper

1 Bring all the liquids to the boil and then leave them to reduce slowly.
2 Add the shallots and garlic and all the other ingredients. Bring to the boil and leave to simmer for 30 minutes. Taste and serve.

Notes
• Since this is a basic, informal sauce, you could use orange squash instead of fresh orange juice.

Tomato Fondue

Tomato fondue is a very basic, clean-tasting, tomato sauce, made without any purée or thickening agents: it's just pure and fresh-tasting. It is a very good sauce for vegetarians and another basic sauce to which you can add a variety of additional flavours. It is one of the first sauces I teach at my cookery school, because of its versatility.

A *Beurre Blanc* (page 110) added in equal quantities, makes a wonderful tomato *beurre blanc*, and has terrific depth of flavour. Tomato *sabayon* can be made with the *sabayon* recipe and about 1 ladle of Tomato Fondue to three or four egg yolks. You could also blend it with Fish *Velouté* Sauce (page 107). What I am saying, basically, is that it is suitable for anything in which you want a rich, tomato flavour to come through.

The word *fondue* comes from the French word *fondre*, to melt, hence its other application to the traditional Swiss fondue. This is really what we're doing here, allowing the tomatoes to melt into a thick sauce. Always remember to season tomato dishes with a lot of salt, at the end of the preparation. Tomato fondue freezes quite well, and keeps well in the refrigerator for at least a week. It is a good stand-by sauce, which you can serve with pasta, fish or meat.

SERVES 6

1 large onion or 2 shallots, sliced
2 garlic cloves, peeled and crushed
25ml olive oil
750g tomatoes, peeled and quartered
100ml white wine or medium sherry
salt and pepper
handful of fresh basil leaves, *chiffonaded* (finely shredded)

1 Sweat the onion and garlic, until soft, in the oil. Do not let them colour.
2 Mix the tomatoes with the onion and garlic and stir in the white wine or sherry slowly, stirring all the time.
3 Cook the mixture on a medium heat for about 25 minutes, until the tomatoes are soft and have broken down. Stir occasionally.
4 Blend the mixture in a food processor for about 3 minutes. Pass through a sieve into a clean saucepan. Season and finish with the fresh basil just before serving.

Notes

• For extra sweetness, make a gastric, a sweet-and-sour addition. Simply mix 60ml each of caster sugar and white-wine-vinegar. Reduce this mixture by half and stir it into the sieved fondue.

• Remember to keep the fresh basil back until you are about to serve; do not stir into the sauce or it will lose its colour.

• Fresh herbs like basil will hold their colour for a short time once chopped if you sprinkle a little salt over them.

Beurre Blanc

This is a basic recipe for many other sauces, which you can create by adding a multiplicity of flavourings to the reduction.

SERVES ABOUT 8

1 dessertspoon white wine vinegar
2 dessertspoons white wine
2 shallots, finely chopped
1 lemon grass stalk, chopped (optional)
6 whole black peppercorns
250g unsalted butter, chilled and cut in 1cm cubes
   or small slices
juice of half a lemon or lime
salt and pepper

1 Put the vinegar, wine, shallots, lemon grass (if using) and peppercorns in a deep saucepan over a low heat and leave to reduce to a syrup, which will take about 10 minutes; this is known as the reduction.

2 Gradually whisk the chilled butter into the reduction, piece by piece, until it melts and amalgamates into a sauce.
3 Pass the sauce through muslin (or a fine sieve) into a clean saucepan or other container. Season and add lemon or lime juice to taste. Keep the sauce warm, so it does not set solidly.

Notes
• The lemon grass is optional, although it does add significantly to the flavour. The sauce is best kept at room temperature, so that it doesn't set; be careful to re-heat it gently, on a low heat, or it will separate.
• Various flavours, such as orange, tomato, pepper and so on, can be added to stage 1 (the reduction) and then again, in purée form, to enhance the flavour at stage 3.
• If the sauce does chill and set, you can still use it by making another reduction and adding the set sauce little by little, whisking continuously until amalgamated.

Vierge Sauce

A knowledge of the French language helps in this recipe! *Une vierge* is a virgin and reflects the use of virgin (ideally extra virgin) olive oil in the sauce. *Chiffonade* comes from the word *un chiffon*, a rag. When preparing the herbs *chiffonade*, you are crumpling and slicing them very gently and finely. When you've done this, season them with a little salt, to preserve the colour.

This is similar to the Antiboise Sauce (page 104), but we're adding a lot more herbs and lemon juice and the extra virgin olive oil. Sauce *Vierge* is brilliant with fish and excellent as a starter sauce. Served fresh, it is green and interesting, with lots happening in terms of appearance and flavour. It does keep well in the refrigerator but don't add the herbs if you're going to store it, as they will go black; add them only when you're about to use the sauce.

Oily sauces have become very popular; the extra virgin olive oil adds a Mediterranean feel to the dish.

SERVES 6

100ml extra virgin olive oil
2 garlic cloves, crushed to a paste
3 shallots, finely chopped
30ml freshly squeezed lemon juice
2 tomatoes, *concassé* (page 25)
6 fresh basil leaves, cut in a fine c*hiffonade***
   (shredded finely)
12 fresh coriander leaves, cut in a fine *chiffonade*
1 tablespoon chopped fresh chives
salt and pepper

1 Heat the oil gently and add the garlic and shallots; simmer until they become soft and translucent.
2 Add the lemon juice, tomatoes and herbs. Serve immediately.

Notes
• A little balsamic vinegar will add piquancy; you could also add stoned black and green olives for extra flavours.

Teriyaki Sauce

This recipe was given to me by a Japanese friend. As I understand it, teriyaki sauces vary incredibly, depending on where in Japan you are and where you were trained to cook. My friend's restaurant was in Birmingham! The secret is in the rice vinegar and the way that it is very gently heated.

The lemon grass cut in half lengthways adds a very good flavour, leaving the stalk in two pieces lets the flavour out and still allows you to remove it easily after cooking. This is very good as a dipping sauce or for stir-fry dishes. It is also excellent for a barbecue, brushed on to fish or meat before they are grilled.

SERVES 6

150ml soy sauce (about 1 small oriental bowlful)
1 dessertspoon rice vinegar
2 garlic cloves, crushed
1 small green chilli, de-seeded and finely chopped
1 small bunch of spring onions, finely chopped
4 slices of fresh root ginger, peeled and finely chopped
stalk of lemon grass
salt and pepper

1 Add the garlic to the soy sauce and vinegar.
2 Add the chilli to the mixture, with the ginger, lemon grass and spring onions. Allow the flavours to infuse for a few hours and then re-heat gently. Always check the seasoning before serving, and remove the lemon grass stalk.

Notes

• You can pass the sauce through a sieve, to leave a black clear sauce which is similar to that which you would buy in the shops, but I prefer to see the ingredients in it.
• Whichever method you choose, make sure that the ingredients are finely and neatly chopped. You can even finish with a chopped fresh herb.
• Soy sauce, rice vinegar, chilli and garlic will vary quite a bit in intensity of flavour, so adjust the quantities above, if necessary, and always taste until you are satisfied.

Indian Marinade

This is an idea that you keep up your sleeve and use occasionally. It is ideal with lamb, chicken or even fish. Marinate for at least 24 hours.

I haven't specified the quantity of coriander, as it does depend on your taste. About two large sprigs for six chops would be about right; you really do want the taste of it in the marinade.

half a teaspoon ground cloves
1 teaspoon ground cumin
1 teaspoon ground turmeric
4 cardamom pods
150ml olive oil
1 garlic clove
2 shallots
sprigs of fresh coriander
4 slices of fresh root ginger or 1 teaspoon ground ginger
salt and pepper

Mix all the ingredients together and add the meat, chicken or fish. Allow to marinate for 24 hours.

Notes
- If you can't get fresh coriander, ground coriander can be used. It doesn't taste anything like the same but you still get a nice flavour. The marinade can be stored in the refrigerator for a long while but be warned, the flavour becomes stronger the longer you leave it. After a week it's quite strong!

Oriental Marinade

This is ideal for marinating meat for barbecues. Like Indian Marinade, it can be stored in the refrigerator for a long while but gains in strength over time. Using it after a couple of days is ideal.

1 tablespoon Chinese five-spice powder
75ml soy sauce
2 garlic cloves, chopped
3 spring onions, chopped
30ml dry white wine
4 slices fresh root ginger
20g sugar
30ml sesame oil
1 tablespoon white wine vinegar
freshly ground black pepper

Mix all the ingredients together, pour over the meat, poultry or fish you are marinating and cover with cling film. Refrigerate for 24 hours, to allow all flavours to penetrate.

Saté Sauce

This is a delicious, thick, rich saté sauce, which I got from my mum. She saved me from embarrassment one day, while I was running a summer cooking school. On the syllabus (I think this was a request from the students) was a barbecue. There was I, the barbecue expert, saying we're going to make teriyaki sauce, barbecue sauce, marinades, griddled chicken, meats ... and saté sauce. It was only after my announcement that I realised I didn't have a saté sauce recipe! I knew the principles but couldn't remember the detail. So, as we all do in moments of crisis, I rang my mum.

She had always made a brilliant saté sauce and she gave me this recipe over the telephone. The chief secret is that it's made with fresh unsalted peanuts, ground in the food processor. Also add a little bit of cream, which helps to amalgamate the sauce.

Adjust the seasoning as you like – making it more spicy, perhaps – but be careful to do this at the end. There are a lot of flavours happening here; you don't want to season it and then find, when it's cooked and you can't do anything about it, that you've added too much.

MAKES ABOUT 300ML

1 onion, minced or finely chopped
30ml groundnut oil
125g peanuts, ground
2 garlic cloves, crushed
1 teaspoon chilli powder
1 teaspoon ground coriander
half teaspoon ground cumin
200ml chicken, meat or vegetable stock
30ml light brown sugar
1 tablespoon soy sauce
1 tablespoon lemon juice
100ml double cream
salt and pepper

1 Put all the ingredients (except the cream) into the liquidiser or food processor for a few moments, until you have a fine sauce.

2 Pour the mixture into a saucepan and leave to simmer. Add the cream and cook until the sauce is fairly thick and rich and the flavours have mellowed (usually simmered for 30 minutes).

3 Taste and adjust the seasoning (as well as the lemon juice) before using.

Notes

• Chicken stock could be replaced with wine for quickness but try to match the stock to the meat that you will be serving: chicken stock for saté chicken, meat stock for saté meat and so on.

• The cream can also be substituted with natural yoghurt stirred in at the end of the recipe, when the sauce has had a chance to cool a little (otherwise it will split).

Rouille

This is a good rich, garlicky dish, which takes its lovely yellow colour from the saffron. It works well with fish dishes. We used to serve it with red mullet soup and it was really brilliant.

SERVES 2/MAKES ABOUT ½ LITRE

2 egg yolks
2 pinches of saffron strands
2 garlic cloves, crushed to a paste
100ml white wine vinegar
125ml olive oil
125ml flavourless oil, e.g. grapeseed
1 tablespoon chopped fresh chives (optional)
salt and pepper

1 Put the egg yolks, saffron, garlic and vinegar in a bowl and whisk them together.

2 Add the oil slowly, as you would for Mayonnaise (page 118), until the sauce is thick and yellow.

3 Taste and season and add the chopped chives, if using.

Notes
• You could add chilli to this, for some extra zing. Use one small green and one small red chilli; halve, de-seed and finely chop them, and substitute for chives.

Pesto Sauce

The name *pesto* comes from an Italian word that means 'to pound'. It is essentially a herb ground to a paste. Like most chefs, however, I use *pesto* to mean a basil sauce, one that is often associated with tomatoes and used as a topping for pizza or pasta.

This particular pesto sauce can be added in small quantities (of about a heaped teaspoon) to a *beurre blanc* or cream sauce for excellent results.

FOR 150ML BOWL

large bunch of fresh basil
60g pine kernels, toasted
60g freshly grated Parmesan cheese
1 garlic clove, crushed to a paste
30ml olive oil
salt and pepper

1 Put all the ingredients (except the olive oil and seasoning) in a food processor and blend them to a purée.

2 Add the olive oil gradually, until you have a thickish paste. Season, taste and transfer to an airtight container, for storing in the refrigerator.

Herb Vinaigrette

This is a good way of getting all the flavours into the dressing, by cooking them. You will not get nearly as much flavour in an uncooked dressing. As soon as you cook the garlic, thyme and other herbs into the oil, the flavours start coming out. As soon as you sieve it, you have all the flavour and none of the bits.

SERVES 2/MAKES ABOUT ½ LITRE

250ml olive oil
1 garlic clove, crushed
4 fresh thyme sprigs
2 fresh marjoram sprigs
3 fresh basil leaves
leaves from a tiny sprig of rosemary
50ml white wine (or balsamic) vinegar
150ml cold water
1 tablespoon salt

1 teaspoon caster sugar
1 teaspoon freshly ground white pepper
squeeze of lemon juice
freshly picked soft green herbs, finely chopped

1 In a saucepan, mix together the oil, garlic, thyme, marjoram, basil and rosemary.
2 Bring to simmering point and then draw the pan off the heat.
3 Cover and leave to stand at room temperature for 3 or 4 hours, to allow the flavours to infuse.
4 Using a ladle, force the dressing through a fine conical sieve into a mixing bowl.
5 Whisk in the vinegar, water, salt, sugar, pepper and lemon juice.
6 Add the soft green herbs last, to keep their colours.
7 Taste and correct the seasoning, if necessary.

Tomato Vinaigrette

This is basically a tomato fondue with white wine vinegar and olive oil and finished with a fresh herb and chopped tomato. Very simple; very good.

MAKES ABOUT 150ML

50ml Tomato Fondue (page 109) or tomato juice
pinch of salt
pinch of caster sugar

dash of white wine vinegar
100ml extra-virgin olive oil
white pepper
chopped fresh basil
2 tomatoes, *concassé* (page 25)

1 Add the first four ingredients to the olive oil, whisk them in, season and taste.
2 Add the basil and tomatoes and serve.

Cooked Vinaigrette

Cooking a vinaigrette gives the flavours a better chance to infuse into the oil. This will be really tasty as a salad dressing or, re-warmed, as a sauce on various starters. If you add a little red wine after the vinaigrette is cooked, it gives a good colour.

MAKES ABOUT 1 LITRE

250ml olive oil
150ml white wine
85ml white wine vinegar
75g carrots, finely chopped
75g celery, finely chopped
75g onion, finely chopped
50g leeks, finely chopped
50g fennel, finely chopped
peel of 1 orange
12 black peppercorns
1 bay leaf
2 fresh rosemary sprigs
2 fresh thyme sprigs
2 fresh tarragon sprigs
2 fresh parsley sprigs
1 tablespoon sugar
4 garlic cloves, finely sliced
chopped fresh chives
salt and pepper

1 Mix the olive oil, wine and vinegar in a thick-bottomed saucepan.
2 Add the rest of the ingredients except the chives, bring to the boil and cook for 20 minutes, to allow the flavours to intensify and infuse into the mixture.
3 Allow to rest and cool, and then pass through a muslin-lined *chinois* (conical) strainer into a clean container. Store in screw-topped bottles and refrigerate.
4 Season and add chopped fresh chives to taste before using. You can do this each time you take some from the bottle, in order that you only season what you actually need.

Notes

• If you have stored this make sure you shake your container well before use.
• You could also use this as a herb dressing, adding about 50g Provençal herbs with all the other vegetables and herbs. This is a very popular dressing at the Pink Geranium.

Mayonnaise

Do not use a scented oil for this recipe as it will affect the flavour; vegetable oil is best. Dijon mustard can be replaced with English. It is a basic sauce for various dips, which can be produced by adding saffron, chopped herbs, crushed garlic or any flavourings that you like. If you are adding extras, do so after stage 3.

MAKES ABOUT 250ML

2 egg yolks
1 teaspoon Dijon mustard
1 teaspoon white-wine vinegar
2 teaspoons lemon juice
300ml best quality, non-scented oil
salt and pepper

1 In a mixing bowl, put the egg yolks, mustard, vinegar and lemon juice.

2 With a hand or electric whisk, slowly trickle in the oil and allow the sauce to thicken, eventually taking all the oil. Add the oil a drop at a time at first, increasing the quantity gradually as the mayonnaise thickens until you're adding it in a thin, slow, steady stream.

3 Season to taste and serve.

Notes

• Everyone is always worried about preventing mayonnaise from separating; in fact, the risk of separation isn't so great, provided that you take reasonable care in adding the oil, especially at first.

• If the worst happens, adding a little boiling water can often rectify the situation. If not, start again with more egg yolk, mustard, vinegar and lemon juice and add the curdled mixture a little at a time.

Mustard Vinaigrette with Green Peppercorns

This is an interesting contrast with Herb Vinaigrette (page 116), because it's uncooked. The flavours will be more obvious, less subtle. To my mind, less appealing, but the recipe takes less time, of course, and is served cold.

MAKES ABOUT 300ML

2 teaspoons green peppercorns in brine
1 teaspoon Dijon mustard
large pinch of salt
25ml olive oil

1 tablespoon white-wine vinegar
1 tablespoon chopped fresh chives

1 Crush half the green peppercorns to a paste with the blade of a knife and put them into a bowl, with the mustard and salt. Pour in half the oil in a slow trickle, whisking continuously until the mixture thickens.

2 Add a little vinegar and slowly trickle in the rest of the oil. Finally, add the remaining vinegar.

3 Pass through a fine conical sieve and add the remaining green peppercorns.

4 Add the chopped chives, taste and serve.

Crème Chantilly

Crème Chantilly is a sweetened cream that works as a good garnish for something that has a sharp taste, like lime tart. It's also an ideal filling for *petits fours* (chocolate cases and tartlets).

2 vanilla pods
600ml double cream
icing sugar, to taste

1 Remove the seeds of the vanilla pods with the back of a small knife and add them to the cream. Discard the pods.
2 Whisk the cream until softly thick. Add a little icing sugar, whisk it in and taste. Add more sugar, if necessary, and whisk until the cream holds a peak. Serve immediately.

Notes

• You can make a good soured cream by whipping the double cream until it's softly thick and then adding the juice of one lemon and a pinch of salt; taste this and continue to whisk until the cream almost holds a peak – although I'm not suggesting this as a pudding garnish!

Caramel Sauce

This is a good alternative to Butterscotch Sauce (page 121).

MAKES ABOUT ½ LITRE

500ml double cream
500g caster sugar
100ml cold water

1 Heat the cream gently. Separately, heat the sugar with the water over a medium heat in a thick-bottomed, straight-sided metal saucepan, stirring to dissolve the sugar. Continue cooking, until the mixture turns to a good caramel colour, without allowing it to burn. The temperature on a sugar thermometer should be 160°C. If you brush cold water round the top of the caramel pan with a pastry brush, that will prevent sugar from crystallizing around the pan.
2 Add the heated double cream.
3 Pass through a sieve and allow to cool before use.

Crème Anglaise

Crème Anglaise is a custard sauce. The secret is that we use double cream and milk together for richness. You must be careful when you put it on the heat; keep beating it with the spoon. If the heat catches it, it will separate, so watch it all the time. The cream helps to stop it separating too easily.

There are many versions of this custard recipe but this one is the best, in my opinion. I particularly like its creamy and smooth texture.

SERVES ABOUT 8

1 vanilla pod
6 egg yolks
100g caster sugar
225ml milk
225ml double cream

1 Split the vanilla pod and take out the seeds with the back of a small knife. Reserve the pod. Add the seeds to the egg yolks and whisk them with the sugar, until light, frothy and doubled in size.

2 Add the vanilla pod to the milk and cream mixture and bring this to the boil, carefully, in a thick-bottomed saucepan.

3 Pour the cream/milk mixture into the egg yolks, whisking continuously. Return to the milk saucepan, stirring continuously, and heat gently until the mixture thickens and coats the back of a wooden spoon.

4 Remove from the heat, pass through a sieve (which will extract the vanilla pod) into a clean container and leave to cool before use.

Notes
• It might be advisable to put the sauce at stage 4 directly into an iced container, to cool it rapidly and further reduce the possibility of separation.
• You can add many flavours to this custard sauce, including liqueurs, coffee and chocolate (mocha), cinnamon, orange or other citrus juices and so on.

Crème Pâtissière

Crème Pâtissière is a thick Crème Anglaise, or custard, thickened with flour. It makes an extremely good base for a soufflé or use it as a filling for flans or tartlet cases.

SERVES ABOUT 10

6 egg yolks
80g caster sugar
1 vanilla pod
400ml milk
50g plain flour, sifted

1 Put the eggs yolks and sugar in a medium-size bowl. Split open the vanilla pod with a small knife and add the seeds to the bowl. Reserve the pod. Whisk the egg yolks and sugar until creamy (this mixture is called a sauce sabayon in French or zabaglione in Italian).
2 Bring the milk to the boil, with the vanilla pod.
3 Add the flour to the egg and sugar mixture and briskly stir it in, until it's well mixed.
4 Pour on the boiling milk, whisking until smooth. Put the mixture back in the saucepan. Cook over a gentle heat, allowing the eggs to cook and thicken the sauce. This will take 5-10 minutes. Sieve and allow to cool before using.

Notes

• The high ratio of egg yolks to flour 'cooked out' at stage 4 makes this Crème Pâtissière a richer, smoother version than you may find elsewhere.

Butterscotch Sauce

This is a recipe we've perfected over the years. It is easy to do and it's rich and sticky, with loads of calories, and absolutely delicious. This sauce can successfully be re-heated, so make it in advance and store it in the fridge. It will keep for a week.

SERVES ABOUT 10

300g unsalted butter
500g demerara sugar
225ml double cream

1 Melt the butter and sugar together and boil gently for about 15 minutes, until it starts bubbling and browning and begins to caramelize.
2 Remove the pan from the heat and stir in the double cream. Pass the sauce through a sieve, to extract any lumps, and allow it to cool.

Notes

• This sauce works well with the Strawberry Soufflé (page 94), and of course the Hot Banana Soufflé, as well as with many other puddings and ice creams.

Coulis

A coulis is a fine fruit purée, made by blending soft fruit with a little sugar stock syrup (sugar and water, as described below). Most soft fruit can be used: strawberries, raspberries, blackcurrants, blackberries, blueberries and redcurrants are all ideal.

MAKES ABOUT 300ML

75g caster or icing sugar
150ml water
250g soft fruit
juice of half a lemon

1 Make a sugar stock syrup, by dissolving the caster sugar in the water. Bring this to the boil but do not allow the syrup to colour.

2 Blend the fruit with the stock syrup in a food processor, until it is smooth and light.

3 Pass through a sieve (preferably a nylon one), using the back of a ladle to extract as much juice as possible into a clear container; chill. Add the lemon juice just before serving, to bring out the flavours of the fruit.

Vegetarian Dishes and Accompaniments

A good chef will cook everything well, including a vegetarian dish! I say this because I've often heard chefs say, 'I'm not a vegetarian myself, so that explains why I can't cook it' – and it doesn't. Good chefs have a vast knowledge of food, flavours, marriages, colours and textures, and this expertise should come into play in a big way with vegetarian food. A good example of this is my vegetarian gâteau, which looks identical to the crab gâteau (page 26), but without the crab and with the addition of herbs and pimentoes to make a superb dish. Soufflés also look very impressive, and as if a lot of time and thought has gone into them.

No-one should feel an afterthought, vegetarians included, and it's worth your time and effort to devise something for all your guests – as a restaurateur I know a plate of vegetables or a salad is simply not good enough. Take time to think about the various vegetable uses I have described throughout the book, and learn to create something with care. Mediterranean, pickled, marinated and chargriddled flavours make a welcome change for all palates. Here follow a few ideas.

Savoury Stilton Soufflés
with tarragon sauce

People generally panic at the thought of making a soufflé. I frequently watch with curiosity the way that some cooks carefully open the oven door and pray that it is rising! Making a soufflé is not a difficult task, nor is it difficult to guarantee its lightness and flavour. So let's take a few moments to look at the secrets of success.

The soufflé dish is of premium importance in ensuring success. You should find ramekin dishes that are ovenproof and have deep, straight sides (a dish with slanting sides will not work). When you have found suitable dishes, brush them with melted butter with a pastry brush, using even, circular, clockwise movements around the sides, carefully painting on the butter in tidy strokes. Then repeat this for the bottom of the dishes and put them in the refrigerator to set. After 20 minutes or so, remove them and butter them again in exactly the same way; dust with finely-grated Parmesan cheese and refrigerate again. This will ensure that the soufflé mixture rises evenly and easily.

From time to time, open the oven and give the dishes a quarter or a half turn. This will help the soufflé to rise evenly, because no oven is exactly the same temperature all over. Do not be afraid of opening the oven; a good soufflé can withstand a few interruptions, providing that they are carefully executed: no banging the door! If you find the soufflé has stuck to one side of the dish, use a palette knife to prise it away carefully, allowing it to rise evenly. You should be careful to touch only the sticking side.

Always fill the soufflé dish to the top with the mixture and then wipe the top with the flat of a palette knife, to smooth the top surface evenly. If the dish is filled to its maximum, the mixture will rise to its maximum. Ovens vary considerably and, if you find that yours is browning the soufflé too much before it is actually cooked, turn it down moderately and keep a watch on it from then on.

When serving the soufflé, it is a good idea to make a separate sauce and, after serving, pierce the soufflé top with a teaspoon and pour the sauce into the centre. This will add extra flavour and the soufflé should bubble and rise a little further in front of your guests.

For the soufflés:

30g unsalted butter
30g plain white flour
150ml milk
3 egg yolks
lemon juice
125g Stilton cheese, grated
8 egg whites
pinch of salt
2 tablespoons chopped fresh chives
salt and pepper

For the tarragon sauce:

60ml dry white wine or sherry
250ml double cream
large bunch of fresh tarragon, chopped
salt and pepper

For the soufflés:

1 Preheat the oven to 220°C/425°F/Gas Mark 7 and prepare the soufflé dishes as above. Make the soufflé base by first melting the butter in a deep saucepan. Sift in the flour and stir well with a wooden spoon to form a *roux*.

2 Gradually add the milk, stirring (or whisking) all the time, until the mixture becomes smooth. Then add the egg yolks, with a few drops of lemon juice, and stir them in, followed by the grated cheese. Season to taste and allow to cool.

3 Whisk the egg whites with the salt until they're stiff; add some lemon juice to help stiffen.

4 Fold the egg whites into the soufflé base, adding the chopped chives. Divide between the prepared dishes.

5 Bake for about 15 minutes, or until they are golden brown and well risen.

For the tarragon sauce:

1 In a deep saucepan, reduce the white wine and then add the double cream; bring to the boil and simmer until smooth, thick and creamy.

2 Season to taste.

3 Just before the sauce is served, add some chopped, fresh tarragon leaves. Allow to infuse a little (off the heat) before serving.

 Alsace Gewürztraminer.

Wild and Forest Mushrooms
with coriander noodles and truffle-oil dressing

This is a simple but brilliant starter. Mushrooms are delicious when just simply pan-fried and seasoned and the noodles taste like no other noodles you'll ever have, if you follow the simple recipe for the pasta, with lots of coriander and chives.

The flavours are excellent and the presentation can be stunning, with the coriander noodles sitting in the middle of the plate to give height. The noodles can be blanched in advance, so all you do is re-heat them; the mushrooms could also be pre-seared, which then just leaves you with the construction of the dish to finish at the last minute.

This can be served with other sauces and you could add to the dish pan-fried calf's liver with fewer mushrooms, putting three pieces of calf's liver around the noodles.

At the restaurant, we would see this as a daily menu dish rather than an á la carte one but, when I've served it at home for dinner parties, people think it looks very impressive and tastes fantastic.

SERVES 4

500g assorted mushrooms
200g Coriander Noodles (page 174)
olive oil
20ml dry Madeira or sherry
25g unsalted butter, melted
salt and pepper

For the dressing:
15ml truffle oil
10ml balsamic vinegar
chopped fresh chives
chopped fresh coriander
1 dessertspoon extra virgin olive oil

1 Clean and pick over the mushrooms and wipe them with a damp cloth; do not wash them.

2 Make and pre-cook the Coriander Noodles.

For the dressing:
Mix the truffle oil and vinegar together and season to taste; truffle oil is very aromatic and can be over used, so be careful not to overpower the flavours of the wild mushrooms. Finish with some chopped fresh chives and coriander, a dessertspoonful of olive oil, and season.

To cook the mushrooms:
1 Pour a little olive oil into a very hot frying-pan on the stove.

2 When the oil starts to smoke slightly, add the mushrooms and stir or toss them regularly, until they become tender.

3 At this stage, add the Madeira to de-glaze the pan (bringing together the flavours); season and taste.

To serve:
1 Warm the noodles in a saucepan with the butter and a serving spoon of boiling water; season them.

2 Make a pasta tower (see page 174) and serve the mushrooms around it, being careful to select a good variety of kinds for each serving.

3 Add the truffle dressing by carefully spooning it over and around the mushrooms. Serve immediately.

A good Macon or classy Italian like Vigna di Gabri.

Notes

• Finding suitable mushrooms may be a problem. If you have a choice, try shiitake, girolles, trompettes, brown cap and oyster mushrooms. Ask at your greengrocer or delicatessen what mushrooms are available.

• Note also that wild and forest mushrooms should be wiped and picked clean, but should never be washed as they lose both texture and flavour and also absorb unwanted moisture.

• You can change the truffle dressing for any of the other dressings that I suggest in the chapter on sauces.

Risotto of Mushrooms
with Stilton and spinach

Stilton has a distinctive taste and, if you're not keen on it, replace it with almost any other cheese. I sometimes cook this recipe without the Stilton and spinach and do mushroom risotto, or I leave out the mushrooms and include just the cheese and spinach. You can play around with this basic recipe idea to suit your own taste.

The secret has to be the rice and how it's cooked. There are various different types of Italian short-grain risotto rice available, although I tend to use arborio rice, which is the most common. The key is to sweat the rice first, in a little olive oil, garlic and shallots. This way, you're starting to get the flavours into the rice right from the start. You must then add the stock a bit at a time, waiting for each addition to be absorbed before adding any more; if you do this you can be sure of producing something that is very different from standard boiled rice.

If you want a very strong mushroom flavour, make a mushroom stock out of the trimmings and stalks, and add this to the risotto instead of the vegetable stock.

SERVES 4

For the risotto:
3 shallots, finely chopped
1 garlic clove, crushed
about 100ml olive oil
300g risotto rice
200ml white wine
450ml Vegetable Stock, warmed (page 102)
450g assorted mushrooms, picked over, wiped and sliced
100g Stilton or other cheese
salt and pepper

To serve:
250g spinach, cooked (page 175)
chopped fresh coriander or tarragon (optional)

1 Sweat the shallots and garlic in half the olive oil until tender; add the rice and sweat it for 2 minutes.

2 De-glaze by adding the white wine to the pan (this brings the flavours together) and leave it to reduce to a syrupy consistency.

3 Now add half the stock and bring it to the boil.

4 Meanwhile, fry the mushrooms in a very hot frying-pan, in the remaining oil.

5 Add the remaining stock to the risotto and bring it to the boil again. Leave to simmer for 6-8 minutes, or until it thickens and the rice cooks through; the grains should be soft but not soggy.

6 Add the cheese and seasoning to taste and then add the cooked mushrooms.

7 Add the coriander to the risotto.

8 Put a bed of spinach on each plate. Using a large straight-sided metal pastry ring, mould the risotto into a neat shape on the bed of spinach.

 Chianti, or Italy's fabulous Tancredi.

Notes

• Adding a potato galette (page 90) on the top works really well; the flavours and textures together are very good. I hesitated at first about putting potatoes with rice, because they are both carbohydrate-rich, but adding the galette really does make the dish look finished.

• The classic sauce to accompany this as a main course would be *Beurre Blanc* (page 110), but you could try *Sauce Vierge* (page 111), Antiboise Sauce (page 104) or anything vegetarian, even a rich garlic or herb cream, but remember to use double cream and to reduce it, allow the flavours to infuse. Finally, you could garnish this with some Roasted Vegetables (page 180).

Rösti Potatoes

Rösti is one of my favourite potato dishes: hence it's used frequently in the book. I was once asked by the producer of *Ready Steady Cook* to use another type of potato for a change!

I particularly like the crispness and flavours of rösti. Ensure the rösti is well seasoned, and the paprika gives it a caramelized flavour and colour. Rösti is very quick to cook, because it's made from grated potato, you can adapt rösti to a host of uses. You could have a vegetable rösti, with grated carrot and other root vegetables all mixed together and cooked in exactly the same way, or an onion rösti. You can make one big rösti in a frying-pan and cut it into wedges. This is very popular with all my family and makes a nice change from roast potatoes. The Swiss put lots of flavours into their rösti, including speck (salted and cured belly of pork, so not so suitable for vegetarians!), which is delicious.

SERVES 4

2 large baking or chipping potatoes
2 teaspoons paprika
oil, for frying
salt

1 Peel the potatoes (do not wash them) and grate them on to a clean tea towel.

2 Season well with salt (which helps to extract the juices and starch) and then squeeze the grated potatoes in the cloth over a bowl or sink, to remove all the starch.

3 Season the potatoes again, this time with the paprika. Mix the pepper well into the potatoes.

4 Heat a frying-pan with some oil in until it's smoking hot. Using four oiled straight-sided metal pastry rings, pack the potato tightly down with a palette knife. Fry the potato inside the rings (unless you have a pan with a non-stick surface that will damage!).

5 Cook for at least 5 minutes or until the potato starts browning and crispening on the underside; turn them over and repeat for the other side.

6 When the röstis are brown all over, remove them from the pan and reserve on a cooling rack. To re-heat, simply place them in a hot oven for a few minutes.

Notes
• Because rösti is so quick to cook it is ideal for preparing when time is of the essence – or you have forgotten about a potato dish!

Char-griddled Sliced New Potatoes

These are an indispensable accompaniment to fish or to the summer barbecue.

SERVES 4

250g new potatoes
unsalted butter
2 garlic cloves, crushed to a paste
olive oil
salt and pepper

1 Boil the new potatoes in water, with a little seasoning and butter.

2 When they're just tender, refresh under cold running water and leave them to cool. This makes them easier to handle.

3 Slice the potatoes lengthways thinly. Leave them to marinate briefly in a little olive oil and the garlic.

4 Ideally, griddle the slices or fry them in the garlicky oil and arrange them on the plates decoratively.

Mashed Potatoes

The best accompaniment for really rustic-style main courses, such as Guinea-fowl with its own *Confit* and Wild Mushroom Sauce (page 76), or Lamb's Liver and Bacon (page 81).

SERVES 4

6 floury potatoes, peeled and cut in small, evenly-sized
   chunks
50g unsalted butter
25ml olive oil
salt and freshly ground white pepper

1 Barely cover the potatoes with salted water in a saucepan and half the butter. Bring to the boil and cook them until tender. Drain and dry the potatoes off over a low heat, stirring with a wooden spoon. Season and add the remaining butter. Mash the potatoes thoroughly with a potato masher or a potato ricer. Add the olive oil.

2 If you want rosemary-flavoured potatoes, sweat chopped rosemary in the oil, add the wine and reduce until syrupy. Stir into the mash. There are of course all sorts of variations to consider.

3 For a saffron mash, infuse saffron in the white wine for a few minutes and then add to the mash.

Pommes Fondantes

This recipe is sometimes known as *gavroche* potatoes. This is another potato dish I really like. The way of doing these in neat little circles with crisp undersides is very neat and tidy.

At home, I cover the potatoes with a little stock and other flavourings, fresh herbs or spices, and just poach them until they're tender; they absorb the colour of the spices and the stock. They won't glaze or crisp but it's easier to control them and they can then be finished in the oven. They keep well and re-heat very well, so they can be prepared well in advance.

SERVES 4

4 medium-size potatoes
125ml water

100g unsalted butter, chilled and cut in small cubes
salt and pepper

1 Peel the potatoes and square them off. Then, using a 5cm straight-sided metal pastry ring, push the cutter into the potato and trim around the sharp edges of the cut potatoes, to round them off. As you do this, drop the potatoes into the water in a frying-pan, to prevent them from discolouring. Save the trimmings of the potato for mash (page 131).
2 Add the chilled, cubed butter, season with salt and pepper and cook over a low heat, until the water has evaporated and starts to glaze the bottom of each potato.
3 As they glaze, the potatoes will become crisp, so carefully turn them over with a palette knife, until they are golden brown on each side.

Dauphinoise Potatoes

This delicious potato dish works brilliantly with both meat and fish dishes. The garlic and cheese flavours make it almost a dish in itself, but it is especially good with lobster, sea bass and lamb dishes. Here's a very quick version which I often use on *Ready Steady Cook*.

SERVES 2

150ml double cream
1 glass dry white wine
3 garlic cloves, crushed and pasted
1 medium baking potato, peeled and sliced on a mandolin
100g good Cheddar cheese, grated
seasoning

1 Pour the cream into a thick-bottomed saucepan. Add the wine and pasted garlic.
2 Add the sliced potato; bring to the boil, then cover and simmer for 15 minutes, until the potato is tender.
3 Taste and season accordingly. Remove from the pan and press into straight-sided 7cm metal pastry rings. Top each potato with grated cheese, and grill (or blast with a blow torch) to melt the cheese. Remove rings and serve immediately.

Notes

• The addition of sliced onion (1 large onion, chopped) at stage 2 is welcome; I sometimes add freshly chopped coriander or tarragon at in the seasoning at stage 3 for extra flavours.

Griddled Polenta
with wild mushrooms, 'sun-dried' tomatoes and roasted vegetables

To be honest, I am not a great fan of polenta (ground maize), but when it is cooked well it has a good flavour. The problem is when it is cooked badly. The secret is to beat it thoroughly and then make sure it is thoroughly cooked; it must not be grainy.

Once you have your polenta cakes, they offer great versatility. I recommend griddling for that burned effect (both visually and in terms of taste) but grilled with a light touch of oil and herbs is also good.

SERVES 6

For the polenta:
1.2 litres water
pinch of salt
225g polenta flour
60g unsalted butter, melted
120ml olive oil
150ml cooking oil
salt and pepper
60g plain flour

To serve:
450g assorted wild mushrooms, pan-fried (page 126)
6 'Sun-dried' Tomatoes (page 136)
350ml Antiboise Sauce (page 104)

To garnish:
chopped fresh coriander
Roasted Vegetables (page 178)

1 Bring the water to the boil with some salt and pour the polenta into it, stirring until well blended together.
2 Keep stirring and add the melted butter and olive oil.
3 Stir vigorously, until your arm nearly drops off, for about 15 minutes.
4 When the mixture is relatively smooth, season and pour into a greased, shallow baking tray, making a layer 1-2cm thick.
5 Place in the refrigerator and leave to set solidly, for at least 1-2 hours.
6 Preheat the oven to 220°C/425°F/Gas Mark 7. Using a 9-10cm diameter straight-sided metal pastry ring, cut rounds out of the polenta.
7 Heat a char-griddle pan or thick-based frying-pan. Dip the polenta cake into a little flour and fry or griddle in a little oil, to mark or brown each side.
8 Remove the cakes. Bake them to warm them through for 5 minutes.
9 Serve some well seasoned, pan-seared mushrooms, mixed with the sun-dried tomatoes, on top of each of the polenta cakes.
10 Serve the warmed Antiboise Sauce around. Sprinkle with chopped coriander and garnish with roasted vegetables.

WINE South African Pinotage, or Californian Zinfandel (I like Frog's Leap).

Notes
• Be warned, the polenta cakes may stick when fried. Persevere, and take it very gently.
• Apart from the Antiboise Sauce, you could serve *Beurre Blanc* with herbs (page 110) or Tomato Fondue (page 109).

Ricotta and Spinach Ravioli
with basil oil

I did this for the *BBC Good Food* magazine, when I was doing *Good Morning with Anne and Nick* in 1993. It's just a very good vegetarian dish and can be used as a main course or a starter.

The basil oil may sound complicated but it isn't and is much nicer if you make it yourself, though you can buy basil oil from good supermarkets. I topped the dish with Deep-fried Leeks (page 169), to give the dish height.

The secret is to make sure that the egg wash isn't too thin. Roll your pasta with your pasta machine set to size 6, which is normally the penultimate setting, and then use a pastry brush to spread the wash over both sides of the pasta.

Another good tip is to use an oiled, straight-sided metal pastry ring, pushed down on the blunt side, to give shape to the filling.

SERVES 6

400g Pasta dough (page 172)
1 egg yolk, beaten with a drop of milk

For the filling:
250g ricotta cheese
150g spinach, blanched, refreshed in cold water, drained and chopped
half a garlic clove
6 egg yolks
salt and pepper

For the dressing:
large bunch of fresh basil, blanched for a few seconds
small bunch of fresh basil, shredded
200ml light olive oil
salt and pepper

3 plum tomatoes, peeled, de-seeded and finely chopped
salt and pepper

To garnish:
Tomato *Concassé* (page 25)

1 For the dressing, blend the blanched basil, with the olive oil, in a food processor. Ideally, leave to stand in a cool place for 24 hours, so the flavour can develop. Pass the oil and basil mixture through a muslin-lined sieve, pressing it with the back of a ladle to extract all the basil flavour. Discard the basil and bottle the oil.

2 Make the pasta dough.

3 Make the filling by placing the cheese, spinach, garlic and seasoning in a food processor. Process briefly and then set it aside.

4 Pass the pasta dough through a pasta machine, or roll it out thinly on a lightly floured board (see photos **a** and **b**). Cut it into twelve 12cm squares .

5 Add a tiny drop of milk to the beaten egg yolk to make a wash. Brush around the edge of the pasta with a little egg wash (**c**).

6 Put a plain nozzle on a large piping bag. Fill the bag with the spinach and ricotta cheese mixture and pipe into the centre of six pasta squares. (You can also spoon it carefully, see **d**.) Make a well in the middle of each blob of filling (**e**).

7 Carefully place a whole egg yolk in each well. Place an unfilled piece of pasta on top and press around the edge of the square (**f** and **g**), making sure that there are no air bubbles. You could use a straight-sided pastry cutter to hold the edges down (**h**).

8 Use a fluted pastry ring to cut the ravioli. Remove the cutters (**j** and **k**), and brush a little of the egg mixture around the edges to seal, if necessary (**l**). Chill for an hour.

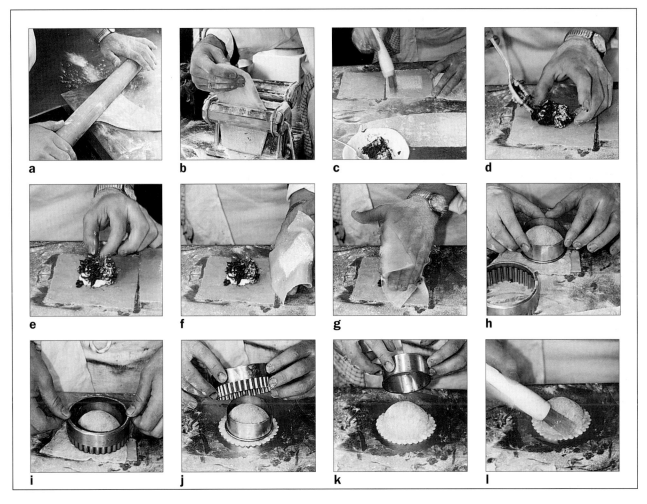

a

b

c

d

e

f

g

h

i

j

k

l

9 To cook, carefully submerge the ravioli in a large pan of boiling, salted water (perhaps with a little olive oil) and cook for just 3 minutes; drain and serve.

10 Meanwhile, gently warm most of the shredded basil and oil in a pan. Pour a little of the oil on to plates or bowls and top with the ravioli. Serve at once, garnished with Tomato *Concassé* and the remaining shreds of basil.

WINE Californian Zinfandel.

Notes

• Serve this with Antiboise Sauce (page 104), Sauce *Vierge* (page 111) or even Tomato Fondue (page 109); it's very flexible. Vinaigrette dressings work well with this dish too and you can use goat's cheese instead of ricotta if you prefer it.

• Deep-fried Leeks (page 169) work brilliantly on top of this.

Blanc
(for keeping white vegetables white whilst cooking)

To keep the white colour of vegetables such as turnips, salsify, Jerusalem artichokes, etc. they need to be cooked in a *blanc*. This is if you are going to poach them – there is no need to do this if you are frying or roasting, of course. The addition of flour, vinegar and lemon juice not only enables the vegetables to hold their colour but also ensures they taste fresh and clean.

900ml water
50g plain white flour
juice of 1 lemon
1 dessertspoon white wine vinegar
1 dessertspoon unsalted butter or olive oil
salt

1 Simply mix all the ingredients together and immerse the white vegetables.
2 Bring to the boil and cook until only just tender.
3 Leave in the *blanc* to cool, for 5 minutes.
4 Drain and dry the vegetables. Re-heat as required.

'Sun-dried' Tomatoes and Peppers

It is easy to dry your own tomatoes and peppers, often with better, fresher results than the bought ones. We do them in the warming cupboard at the restaurant; if you haven't got one of these at home, you can still do them overnight in a really low oven with the door left open. The low oven of Aga-type cookers works beautifully for this.

In the summer, I have dried vegetables at home in the sun, under my fruit nets, so the birds don't get them. If you store them in olive oil they will keep for months, maybe even years. They also look pretty on the shelf in the kitchen, but keep them out of direct sunlight (they're really best kept in the dark). Serve them with things like goat's cheese and in salads, to which they give a wonderful flavour. I'm not a fan of raw peppers, but once they've been dried they are simply delicious.

The method below is for tomatoes, but peppers are treated in the same way, except that they don't need to be skinned.

1-1.5kg plain Italian tomatoes
50g rock salt
12 garlic cloves, finely sliced
fresh thyme sprigs
fresh rosemary
light olive oil

1 Preheat the oven to 100°C/325°F/Gas Mark 1. Skin and de-seed the tomatoes, halve and put them on a baking tray.
2 Sprinkle liberally with the rock salt and add the garlic, thyme and rosemary.
3 Dry in the oven for about 12 hours, or overnight.
4 Remove the herbs, garlic slices and excess salt and put the tomatoes in an airtight jar. Pour on enough olive oil to cover, seal tightly and store in a cool place.

Puy Lentils

These are small, French lentils that don't take a lot of cooking. I include them because they are an excellent accompaniment to a wide range of dishes and also because they don't take as much time to cook as other lentils and pulses. Puy lentils should be cooked *al dente*. The trick is to put lots of flavours into the stock that you are cooking them in.

Lentils and other pulses can be used in millions of different ways: as a bed under meat, game or poultry and as an accompaniment to vegetarian dishes – a change from serving rice or potatoes. At the Pink Geranium, we sometimes do a *cassoulet* of lentils with other beans, served with a tomato fondue with fresh herbs and Mediterranean char-griddled vegetables. This becomes a complete dish, especially topped with some curls of fresh Parmesan cheese. It looks especially good if you mould the lentils and beans into a ring on the plate. Many vegetarians have complimented me on the fact that it is a very tasty dish.

SERVES 4

450g French Puy lentils
100g smoked bacon, cut into small cubes
2 shallots, chopped
3 garlic cloves, halved
star anise and cinnamon stick (optional)
200ml Vegetable Stock (page 102)
75ml red wine
sprig of fresh thyme
salt and pepper

1 In a thick-bottomed saucepan, put all the ingredients and bring to the boil. Allow to simmer for about 20 minutes, until *al dente*. The stock and the red wine should cover the lentils as they cook.

2 Drain off any cooking liquor. Tip the lentils on to a tray to cool, and pick out the garlic, spices and thyme.

Notes
• Add cooked lentils to veal *jus* for a wonderful lentil jus that works brilliantly with lamb dishes.

Pickled Cucumber

This is a refreshing salad that is particularly good with Ceviche of Salmon (page 24). Arrange them in a neat circle on the base of each plate, before placing the ceviche on top. Run the mustard dressing around the cucumber; it looks spectacular.

SERVES 4

1 cucumber
150ml white wine vinegar
60ml dry white wine
2 dessertspoons caster sugar
chopped fresh dill

1 Slice the cucumber thinly, using a mandolin (see page 90), and marinate it in the other ingredients for several hours, to allow the flavours to infuse.
2 Remove the slices of cucumber and dry them, in a tea towel or cloth, to stop the juices running over the plate. Arrange them on each plate in a neat circle.

Notes
• Pickled vegetables (carrots, leeks, celery, fennel, mushrooms etc.) all work well if blanched first, then marinated in a similar marinade to that above, except with half a head (i.e. half of the whole bulb, not just a peeled or crushed clove) of garlic added to it. Use these vegetables to garnish dishes like the Rillette (page 75), Smoked Pigeon (page 17) and those with a *Confit* (page 76).

Garlic *Beignets*

These deep-fried 'puffs' are very easily made.

MAKES ABOUT 12

12 garlic cloves, peeled but left whole
60g unsalted butter
75ml dry white wine
about 60g potato flour
oil, for deep-frying
salt and pepper

1 Bake the garlic cloves, with the butter and wine, in a foil parcel until soft and tender as for Garlic *Confit* (page 170).
2 Process the garlic cloves and cooking juices to a purée, in a liquidiser or food processor.
3 Season the mixture and add potato flour, until it firms up as a spreadable paste.
4 Make quenelles of the mixture, using two teaspoons. Heat the oil for deep-frying to 170°C. If you don't have a deep-fryer, a saucepan containing about 3cm of oil would suffice.
5 Deep-fry two or three quenelles at a time until golden brown, about a minute. Remove and drain. To re-heat, put into a hot oven for a few minutes.

Bread, Batters and Pastry

You can't beat making your own bread. The kitchen will fill with wonderful aromas and leave everyone dreaming of crisp, warm, home-made bread straight from the oven. So it's a shame that few people take the trouble to make their own. The main reason is that some recipes sound complicated and confusing and put a lot of stress on what can go wrong. There is a sort of magic about the chemistry of bread-making ingredients which makes many cooks nervous. Also, making bread isn't an instant process; it does take time, so you need to organise yourself in advance. It seems easier to buy the range of excellent breads now available from supermarkets. The recipes here, however, are better than breads you can buy, and are very simple to make. Your efforts will be well rewarded.

One point to remember is that basic white and brown breads are only the starting point. Once you have exhausted all the various different shapes and sizes you can make basic dough in, you can start experimenting with different flavours. I have recommended both fruit and nut additions to basic doughs. You can also try flavours such as Tapenade (see page 145), chopped herbs, cheese, olives and even sun-dried tomatoes. The recipes are meant to be very adaptable; go ahead and experiment.

This chapter also includes some other classic baked recipes, such as pancakes, and my own recommended method for some useful pastries and other basics, such as my guaranteed never-to-sink method for making Yorkshire pudding.

BREADS AND SAVOURY PASTRIES

White Bread

This is a simple bread that doesn't need much proving, provided that you have a fairly warm kitchen, because it contains a fairly high proportion of yeast. The all-important proving process entails leaving the dough to rest, during which time the yeast will cause it to double in size. (Dried yeast, if you use it, may take longer to prove.) Firstly, you make a 'starter', which comprises a fermented mixture of a little of the flour, warm water and yeast. Once this has fermented, you mix in the other ingredients before leaving the dough to prove.

One useful trick to use before this second stage is to make a cross on top of the dough, which will let more air into the bread. However, since you don't want the dough to dry out either, put cling film over the top and tuck it in around the edges. Leave it in the warm kitchen to expand, until it doubles in size.

The next stage, in classic bread-making, is to knead the dough again, before making it into loaves or rolls. I sometimes leave out this second stage, if I feel the proving has been entirely successful and the dough is ready. If you pull it off in pieces at this stage, rather than the traditional knocking back and second proving, the final bread will come out much lighter.

The reason for putting the rolls at the top of a hot oven, instead of in a warm oven, is to prevent any further proving. You need the rolls to cook at the size you want, not to get any bigger. In a hot oven, you will find they will be brown and crisp and you can serve them straight away.

MAKES ABOUT 20 ROLLS OR 2 LOAVES

850g strong white flour
20g fresh yeast
500ml warm water
20g salt
30g olive oil or unsalted butter
1 egg, lightly beaten
20ml milk

1 Allow 150g of the flour, the yeast and the water to ferment for 15 minutes. This is called a 'starter'.
2 Mix and knead the starter with the remaining flour, salt and oil or butter. Put the dough on a clean worktop and cut a cross in the centre. Cover the dough with cling film and leave to prove for 20 minutes, or until the dough has doubled in size.
3 Pull pieces of the dough away and form into rolls on a good flat surface. Do not use extra flour unless absolutely necessary, as this will make rolling more difficult, and add unwanted flour to the recipe. Put the rolls on a greased and floured surface to avoid sticking. For loaves, divide the dough in two and form the halves into round shapes. Put them on greased baking trays. Or grease and flour two 1kg loaf tins and put the dough in them. Leave the dough to stand for 10 minutes. Preheat the oven to 220°C/425°F/Gas Mark 7.
4 Mix the egg with the milk, to make an egg wash.
5 Baste the rolls or loaves with the egg wash and bake at the top of the oven until they are golden brown. They will be cooked when they sound hollow when tapped underneath.

140 CHEF'S SECRETS

Brown Bread

Many of the recipes in this book are unique to us: I use them regularly in the restaurant and want to share them with you. This recipe is one that I use frequently, at work, for friends and for the family. I prefer to make rolls with this dough, because it leaves out the starter (see White Bread method), which saves time.

The secret of its success, and this is something of a paradox, is that it uses a high ratio of white flour to brown flour. This produces its characteristic lightness. Wholemeal or brown flour is quite heavy and it can be stodgy; the added white flour makes it lighter without losing the brown-bread texture and flavour.

MAKES ABOUT 20 ROLLS OR 2 LOAVES

575g white strong flour
200g wholemeal strong flour
20g salt
20g fresh yeast
500ml warm water

1 Sift the white flour into the brown and then add the salt.
2 Put the yeast in a measuring jug with the warm water and stir this well. When the yeast is diluted, pour it on to the flour.
3 Mix to make a dough and then take the dough out of the bowl and knead it until it's firm, about 5 minutes. Allow the dough to rest on the work surface, covered completely with cling film to stop it from drying out.

4 When the dough has doubled in size, remove the cling film. (This process should take 45 minutes to 1 hour, depending on the heat of your kitchen. If it is quite cool, try putting the covered dough in the airing cupboard.) Pinch off pieces of dough weighing about 35g and roll these into dinner rolls. Alternatively, divide the dough in two and lay the pieces in greased and floured loaf tins. Allow the rolls or loaves to prove again for about 30 minutes in your warm kitchen. Preheat the oven to 230°C/450°F/Gas Mark 8.
5 When it has risen again (it doesn't need to double in size), dust the dough with a little white flour and bake near the top of the oven for about 20 minutes, or until brown. Tap the base to see if it is cooked; it should sound 'hollow'.

Notes

• When you roll the bread, it's important that the surface is not too floury, because you need both warmth and friction. I try to work on stainless steel, which helps to give a bit of friction. The warmth comes from taking the rolls up into the palm of your hand as you move the dough around.
• Another tip, if you are making rolls, is to pinch the dough pieces off and to weigh them: about 35g is ideal. This doesn't take long and gives continuity of size.
• The bread can be rested and re-heated or even frozen (once cooked) successfully.
• For a nutty bread, use the same recipe and add 250g nuts before the second stage of proving. Make sure the nuts are broken into small pieces to prevent them from sinking down to the bottom.

Brioche

This is a classic recipe, and one that works well for us at the Pink Geranium. Making brioches is not as difficult as people imagine. It's like making any other bread, except that butter and eggs are added to the dough.

MAKES 2 LOAVES

20g fresh yeast
100ml warm water
500g white strong flour
6 eggs
20g salt
30g sugar
250g unsalted butter

1 Dissolve the yeast in the warm water.
2 Sift the flour before mixing it with the eggs, salt, sugar and the warm water/yeast mixture.
3 Cream the butter until it is soft and add this to the mixture.
4 Pour the mixture into a clean, deep bowl, cover with cling film to prevent a crust from forming and leave to rest in a warm place for about 45 minutes, or until the dough has doubled in size.

5 When the dough is ready, pour it into well buttered and floured loaf or brioche tins; allow it to prove again until it has reached the height of the tin. Preheat the oven to 180°C/350°F/Gas Mark 4.
6 Bake for about 30 minutes, or until the brioche has risen and turned golden brown.
7 To test whether the brioche is cooked, remove it from the tin and, holding it with a cloth, tap the base; it should sound empty and airy. Remove from the tin and allow it to rest on a cooling rack.

Notes

• I think the secret of making great brioche is to know when it's cooked. It may look cooked: brown and crisp, with the top slightly open as you remove it from the baking tin. However, you need to tap the base of the loaf and ensure that it sounds empty and airy; only then will you know that it really is ready to remove from the oven.
• One other small but important tip is not to skimp on the buttering and flouring of the baking tins.
• To keep brioche fresh when the loaf has cooled, wrap it in cling film and keep it in a cold place. The loaf will keep for some time. Brioche also freezes well.

Pumpkin Bread

Pumpkin bread is a good way of using pumpkin, especially around Hallowe'en, when pumpkins are in abundance and you don't really know what to do with the leftover flesh. I find pumpkin pie a bit uninteresting and I don't really enjoy pumpkin soup either. Pumpkin in bread, though, with the cinnamon and nuts, works brilliantly. It's certainly the best way I know of eating pumpkin. The irony is that it doesn't actually taste like pumpkin at all!

I haven't given pumpkins a very good build-up but this recipe really is worth trying. The bread has a real depth to it; a special character that I'm sure you will enjoy.

MAKES 1 LOAF

1.5kg raw pumpkin flesh, chopped
30g brown sugar
1 teaspoon ground cinnamon
half teaspoon ground ginger
pinch of ground cloves
pinch of salt
125ml vegetable oil
275g white or wholemeal self-raising flour
2 eggs
125g walnuts, chopped

1 Lightly grease a loaf tin and line it with baking parchment. Preheat the oven to 200°C/400°F/Gas Mark 6.

2 Wrap the pumpkin in foil and bake it for 25 minutes. Allow it to cool and then blend the pulp in a food processor.

3 Add the flour, spices and salt, followed by the oil, eggs and nuts. Blend the mixture thoroughly.

4 Allow the dough, covered in cling film, to prove on the work-top until it has doubled in size.

5 Put the dough in the loaf tin to prove again. It will be ready when the mixture rises above the top of the tin.

6 Bake until the loaf is golden brown on top. This will take 50 minutes. The bread should sound hollow when patted on the bottom and then it will slip out of the tin easily. If it sounds at all heavy, return it to the oven.

Notes

• If you find the bread is not ready and you need to return it to the oven, there is, of course, the danger of over-cooking the top. Either put foil over the top, or simply cut it off later. Don't remove the bread from the oven if the inside is still undercooked.

Savoury Shortcrust Pastry

A simple recipe, but shortcrust pastry, properly made, is just as delicious as more unusual pastries. It should be crisp, short and light.

MAKES FOUR 10CM TARTLET CASES OR ONE 20CM TART

250g medium strength plain flour, sifted
1 coffeespoon salt (or ¾ teaspoon)
1 coffeespoon sugar (or ¾ teaspoon)
75g unsalted butter
1 egg yolk, beaten
1 tablespoon cold milk

1 Sift the flour into a mixing bowl, with the salt. Stir in the sugar. Cut the butter in small pieces and add them .
2 Using your fingertips, rub together the dry ingredients and butter until the mixture resembles breadcrumbs. Add the egg and milk. Bring together to make a dough.
3 Wrap in cling film and leave to rest for 1 hour, in the refrigerator.
4 Bake as required in the recipe.

Notes

• It's really quick and easy to make shortcrust in the food processor. Blend softened butter with the egg and gradually blend in the flour and milk.
• The main secret of making shortcrust is to keep all the ingredients, and your hands, as cool as possible. (That's why marble pastry boards are popular.) If the pastry gets too hot, the fat melts and makes it greasy and the finished result won't be so good. For the same reason, try to handle the pastry as little as possible.
• You may need a little more or less liquid to bring the ingredients together as a dough because the end quantity of flour may vary, but always add the minimum you can, and gradually add more if necessary.
• Like other pastries, shortcrust really benefits from being wrapped in cling film and rested in the refrigerator before you roll it out, for approximately 5 hours. This helps the pastry relax and makes it easier to roll out without cracking. I sometimes put it briefly in the freezer, which works beautifully to speed up the process.
• To bake blind, put some greaseproof paper or foil in the pastry case and fill it with ceramic baking beans or dry, hard pulses. Bake for about 15 minutes and then remove the paper and beans and bake for another 5 minutes or so, until the pastry is just starting to colour and crisp and dry on top.

Ciabatta and Tapenade Breads

The delicious flavours of ciabatta bread can be achieved through a few simple modifications of my basic brown bread recipe. This isn't a true ciabatta, as I'm not using Italian flour or proper Italian methods, but you'll see how easy it is to adapt the basic brown bread dough.

MAKES ABOUT TWO LOAVES

575g white strong flour
200g wholemeal strong flour
15g salt
25g fresh yeast
500ml warm water
250g stoned green olives, chopped

1 Sift the white flour into the brown and then add the salt.
2 Put the yeast in a measuring jug, with the warm water and stir well. When the yeast is diluted, pour on to flour. Add olives.

3 Mix to make a dough, then take the dough out of the bowl and knead until firm, about 5 minutes. Then cover the dough completely with cling film to stop it from drying out, and allow to rest on a work surface.
4 When the dough has doubled in size (which will take up to an hour, depending on the heat of your kitchen), remove the cling film. Divide in two and lay each piece in greased and floured loaf tins. Let the loaves prove again for about 30 minutes in a warm kitchen. Preheat the oven to 230°C/450°F/Gas Mark 8.
5 When it has risen again (it doesn't need to double in size), dust the loaves with some white flour, and bake near the top of the oven for about 20 minutes, or until brown.

Notes

• For Tapenade Bread, follow exactly the same method, but use 125g of Tapenade mixture (see page 9) instead of green olives. The flavours of tapenade are so intense that a little goes a long way in getting the olive and anchovy flavours into your dough.

Yorkshire Pudding

Roast beef wouldn't be the same without Yorkshire pudding; it's part of our national heritage. For some reason, Yorkshire pudding has not travelled well, though; it remains a purely British favourite.

Although different regions of Britain favour different styles of Yorkshire pudding, the basic recipe is the same everywhere. The dish is not really a proper pudding, more a soufflé, made from a batter of eggs, milk and flour that is baked until risen, puffy and brown. And wherever you find this old favourite, the same basic problem is always the trouble – how to make the pudding rise and how to keep it risen after cooking.

Most cooks mutter something about the way their grandmothers used to cook Yorkshire pudding, but here is how I ensure a consistently popular version for Sunday lunches at the Pink Geranium. Made in this way, you will be able to keep the puddings warm for some considerable time, without fear of them sinking.

MAKES 10-12 SMALL PUDDINGS

2 eggs, separated
100g plain flour
300ml milk
pinch of salt
vegetable oil

1 Preheat the oven to 220°C/425°F/Gas Mark 8. Pour a little vegetable oil into each hole in a 12-hole Yorkshire pudding tray (or a large Yorkshire pudding dish) and put the tray or dish in the oven to preheat.

2 Beat the egg whites in a bowl until they hold stiff peaks.

3 Mix the egg yolks, flour and milk together, season with salt and then fold in the beaten egg whites.

4 When the oil is smoking hot, pour the batter into the tray or dish, using a small ladle. Put in the middle of the oven for about 15 minutes and don't open the door for the first 10 minutes. It's banging the door that does the real damage, so close it carefully.

5 When the pudding(s) are golden brown on top, you may need to turn them over carefully and cook the bases for a few minutes, to ensure that they are evenly brown and will therefore stay up, even if you have to keep them warm for a while.

Notes

• The technique of stiffly whisking the egg whites and folding them in separately guarantees success. It makes the mixture light and fluffy and helps the rising enormously: so much so that you may need a larger oven!

• It is also very important to ensure that you heat the tray or dish very well before putting the batter in. If the batter doesn't go into smoking hot fat or oil, the outside won't crisp so well, and the puddings are likely to stick to the tins.

Tree Cake

This is probably better known as a butter sponge. I'm not quite sure why we call it this; I think it was the name used by a chef who had worked for the Roux brothers and we've adopted it, though this is our version. This is like any other sponge, except that, obviously, it has butter in it, which makes it a little heavier but more versatile. I use it in particular for lining dishes like Chocolate Marquise (page 162). It also makes a fantastic chocolate roulade by rolling, like a Swiss roll, with the marquise mixture inside.

MAKES TWO 20CM SPONGES

160g unsalted butter
160g sugar
7 eggs, separated
1 vanilla pod
1 dessertspoon double cream
2 dessertspoons rum
160g plain white flour

1 Preheat the oven to 200°C/400°F/Gas Mark 6. Put the butter, sugar and egg yolks in a mixing bowl. Split the vanilla pod open with a small knife and scrape out the seeds into the bowl. Discard the pod. Cream together the butter, sugar, egg yolks and vanilla seeds.

2 Whisk the egg whites until they hold soft peaks. Whip the cream until it holds peaks. Add the rum and then add the cream to the creamed mixture. Finally, fold the egg whites into the creamed mixture.

3 Sift in the flour and fold it in well. Pour into greased and floured cake tins.

4 Bake for about 30 minutes or until golden brown and cooked through. To check if the sponge is cooked, stick a fine skewer into the centre; it should come out clean.

Sweet Shortcrust Pastry and Sweet Shortbread (*Sablé*) Pastry

The orange zest is purely optional. This pastry will need to be prepared at least an hour before use, to allow it to rest. There are many versions of this, but this one, with the addition of double cream, is excellent.

250g plain flour
75g icing sugar
half vanilla pod's seeds (or half teaspoon)
125g unsalted butter, softened
2 egg yolks
120ml double cream (or 2 tablespoons)

1 Mix the flour, sugar and vanilla together. Then add the creamed butter, egg yolks and cream.
2 Bring together by hand until you have a dough. Leave to rest for a few hours, wrapped in cling film in the refrigerator.
3 Bake as required.

Notes
• This can also be made in the food processor, as for Shortcrust Pastry (page 144).
• If you add 50g butter and 10g sugar to this recipe, roll it out to medium thickness, cut it in about 8cm circles and bake them in the oven at 180°C/350°F/Gas Mark 4, you will have excellent *sablés* biscuits; dust them with caster sugar and layer them with fruit and cream for an easy and delicious dessert.

Sweet Pancake (Crêpe) Mixture

2 eggs
1 dessertspoon caster sugar
250ml milk (approx.)
100g plain flour
pinch of salt
dash of olive oil
50ml cooking oil
grated zest of 1 orange (optional)

1 Beat the eggs with the caster sugar. Add the milk and sift in the flour.

2 Add the salt and the cooking oil and orange zest (if using) and pass this mixture through a fine sieve into a clean container, to remove any lumps.

3 Heat a small crêpe pan and then add some oil, enough to coat the base of the pan with a thin film. Heat the oil until it's barely smoking. Using a small ladle, spoon about 2 table-spoons of the batter into the pan. Tilt and rotate the pan to spread the batter evenly, to make perfectly neat pancakes. Cook for 30-60 seconds, or until slightly browned on the underside and then flip the pancake over and cook the other side. Repeat with the remaining batter, re-oiling the pan only as necessary.

Notes

- If you don't have a crêpe pan, use an ordinary frying pan, proved with 1 tablespoon salt – heat the salt (on its own) in the pan for a while on a high heat; discard salt and wipe clean. Then add oil and proceed as normal.
- If you're making crêpes in advance, stack them between squares of greaseproof paper or baking parchment. Re-heat either in the sauce you are serving or in a hot oven (220°C/ 425°F/Gas Mark 7).
- Never wash your pancake pan after use; just wipe it clean with a little oil.
- To make a savoury pancake, omit the sugar and add twice as much salt.

Puddings

I'm afraid I often say on Ready Steady Cook that I hate puddings! In fact, most chefs do, simply because they're terribly time-consuming, and it takes a very patient, specialised chef to work the pastry section of a kitchen. This section, however, is not full of complex recipes, but it is full of simple ideas for successful home entertaining. They are all achievable in a sensible amount of time, and are my favourite selection of desserts that don't mean spending all day in the kitchen.

I've included some good basic recipes in this chapter as well, such as a bread and butter pudding and a recipe for *crème brulée*. I think it's better to produce something 'classic but brilliant' than a complex *nouvelle* recipe which can look very pretty on the plate but be a disaster on the palate!

To be honest, I'm much more of a cheese man myself, although I've recently been recreating the baked cheese recipe (see cooking method page 10), but serving it with a compôte of seasonal fruits (lightly stewed fruits in a *coulis*, page 122, finished like the fruit sauce on page 98). I call this a 'sweese', as it's a really a sweet and cheese in one! My guests adore it, and it makes a refreshing change.

Banana *Glacé*
with *crème de banane* liqueur sauce

Paul, my head chef, came up with this recipe when I asked him to make a pudding using bananas, as I thought that bananas were not used enough in my kitchen. He created this *glacé*, and the flavours are absolutely fantastic. It can be prepared well in advance as it's frozen; it's a great dinner party favourite.

SERVES 12

425g caster sugar
150g shelled hazelnuts
6 egg whites
450ml double cream
7 bananas, mashed

To serve:
100ml *crème de banane* liqueur
Crème Anglaise (page 120)

1 Line individual moulds with greaseproof paper and set the freezer to its coldest.
2 Heat 150g of the sugar in a thick-bottomed pan, to melt it and make a caramel.
3 Stir in the hazelnuts and pour them on to a cold, oiled tray, to set. When cold, crush the hazelnut caramel into small pieces, or blend in your food processor.
4 Whisk the egg whites and the remaining sugar together, to make a stiff meringue.
5 Whip the cream to stiff peaks and then fold it into the meringue. Add the hazelnut caramel and banana and gently fold them in until they are thoroughly mixed.

6 Fill the moulds to the top with the mixture and place in the freezer until hard.
7 Mix the *crème de banane* into the *Crème Anglaise* and allow the flavours to infuse for a few minutes before serving.
8 To serve, remove the moulds from the freezer, rub them briefly with a hot cloth or dip them very briefly in hot water and turn them out. Serve surrounded by *crème de banane-*flavoured *Crème Anglaise*.

 Muscat Beaunes de Venise.

Notes
• This recipe works really well with *Sabayon* Sauce (page 105) as well, infused with the same liqueur and glazed with a blow torch or under the grill afterwards.
• Another interesting way of serving bananas is to make a terrine, by slicing them in half lengthways and covering them in brown sugar and butter and caramelizing the bananas under a hot grill until they just begin to soften, which starts to form a sauce. Then you pack the bananas into the terrine, which has been lined with cling film; make sure all the sauce has been put over the top and put the terrine in the refrigerator to set. When it's turned out, it slices through easily. We used to serve it with a rum *sabayon* or rum cream. It's another easy and wonderfully tasty banana pudding.

My Mother's Terrine of Three Crushed Fruits

I went to a dinner party once at my mother's and she served this; it was excellent. I'm not usually very keen on terrines (I sound grumpy about puddings altogether really!) as I believe that the fruit, or whatever else is going into the terrine, is much nicer left in its natural state. This recipe proves, though, that a terrine can be very successful. It looks pretty, tastes unforgettable and the kiwi fruit sauce, with its tang of lemon, is also brilliant.

My mother, Joy, doesn't like to divulge her recipes but she is an excellent pudding chef, so I managed to persuade this one out of her (see also Saté Sauce, page 114!). She actually prepares some puddings for my brother Stuart's restaurant, The Riverside in Woodbridge, Suffolk. This is a regular on his menu.

SERVES 6

225g strawberries
350g icing sugar
175ml champagne
30g gelatine, dissolved in 150ml water
225g peaches
225g raspberries

For the kiwi fruit sauce:
285g kiwi fruit, peeled and chopped
115g icing sugar
grated zest and juice of half a lemon
120ml sugar stock syrup (see page 122)

1 Rinse a large loaf tin with cold water.
2 Process the strawberries with one third of the icing sugar, one third of the champagne and 50ml of the dissolved gelatine. Sieve this, pour it into the tin and put the tin into the refrigerator to set.
3 Peel and stone the peaches and process them, with another third of the icing sugar, champagne and gelatine; pour this on to the set strawberry layer.
4 Process the raspberries with the remaining icing sugar, champagne and gelatine and pass through a sieve. Pour over the peach layer. Leave in the refrigerator until completely set.
5 To make the kiwi fruit sauce, process the kiwis with the rest of the ingredients and then pass through a sieve.
6 To serve, carefully turn the terrine out and cut it in slices. Pour the sauce on to each plate and serve with a slice of the terrine on the top.

Asti Spumante.

Crisp Pear Tart
with maple syrup ice cream

The puddings I like best are usually quite simple and not too creamy. I like fruit and I like the sweetness of caramel, so this to me is a classic. Everyone has a version of *tarte tatin*; this is a quick version, the secret of which is that you simply put the pears on a base of thinly rolled pastry, put it into the oven and forget about it for 15-20 minutes. It's great if you are entertaining and need a quick pudding. This is the sort of thing I quite often do for a dinner party, if I'm pushed for time.

SERVES 2

about 90g puff pastry
3 pears
60g caster sugar
60g unsalted butter, melted

To serve:
2 portions Maple Syrup Ice Cream (page 166)
2 portions Butterscotch or Caramel Sauce
  (optional, pages 121 and 119)

1 Preheat the oven to 200°C/400°F/Gas Mark 6. Roll out the pastry very thinly (about 2mm thick) and cut it into two rounds, using a side plate for a template. Prick both rounds all over with a fork, to prevent the pastry from puffing up, and put them on a greased baking sheet.

2 Peel and core the pears and slice them very thinly. Arrange the slices neatly in a circle around the puff pastry discs.

3 Sprinkle liberally with the sugar and then pour over the melted butter and bake for about 20 minutes, until crisp.

4 Remove from the oven and serve immediately, with sauce and the maple syrup ice cream melting over the centre.

Notes

• You may have your own preferred puff pastry recipe, otherwise I recommend buying it ready-made. There are several brands available which in my opinion are as good as any you would make yourself. I recommend Sarl François.

• If the pears are very underripe I'd recommend poaching them (peeled and cored), until just tender, in a stock syrup (see page 122), adding cinnamon and white wine to enhance the flavours.

Dark Chocolate Mousse

There are mousses and mousses ... and this is a serious mousse! The secret is the quality of the chocolate that you use. You can't make a silk purse out of a sow's ear and that's certainly true of chocolate recipes; use a premium chocolate if you want a premium result.

SERVES 8

200g dark chocolate with a high cocoa-butter content
6 egg yolks
100g caster sugar
30g freshly ground coffee
1 tablespoon warm water
300ml double cream, lightly whipped

1 Break the chocolate into even pieces and melt them carefully in a glass bowl over a pan of hot, but not boiling, water. It's important that the water doesn't touch the bowl.
2 Meanwhile, whisk the egg yolks and half the sugar in a separate bowl over hot water, until they about double in volume, making a *sabayon*.
3 Mix the coffee, remaining sugar and some water together, to make a syrup. Trickle this on to the *sabayon* and whisk it briskly.
4 Mix this blend into the melted chocolate and add the cream, stir vigorously. Allow to chill and set.

WINE Essencia Orange Muscat from California.

Notes
• You can add about 75ml gently warmed liqueur at step 3, to replace the coffee syrup.
• Having made this delicious mousse once, you can do so much with it. One idea is to pour it into a baking ring, over a sponge that has been soaked in a liqueur; when the mousse is set, turn it out and slice it like a cake. It will also make neat quenelles or you can put it into little dariole moulds lined with cling film. It works well with a mocha sauce (*Crème Anglaise*, page 120, flavoured with chocolate and coffee).
• You can also make a wonderful *mille feuille* with this chocolate mousse. This comprises circles of the same chocolate interspersed with layers of mousse. You melt your chocolate and spread it on cling film stretched over the back of a tray or other flat surface. Spread it with a palette knife, to about the thickness of the palette knife and, once it's set solid (you can even put it in the freezer), cut it into circles with a pastry ring. Put one circle on the plate, pipe some mousse on top, put another chocolate circle on the top and more mousse and then another chocolate circle. Dust this with icing sugar and serve with a mocha sauce. It really is very easy to do and looks out of this world. The name *mille feuille* means 'a thousand leaves' but you will find that three or four are quite sufficient!

White Chocolate Mousse

This won't set without gelatine, and the proportions are different to the dark chocolate mousse. However, the method is the same.

SERVES 8

160g good quality white chocolate
2 leaves gelatine
15ml hot water
150ml double cream

1 Break the chocolate into even pieces and melt them carefully in a glass bowl over a pan of hot, but not boiling, water. It's important that the water doesn't touch the bowl.
2 Meanwhile, soak the gelatine in a little hot water until it has dissolved.
3 Mix this into the melted chocolate and fold in the cream, stir vigorously. Allow to settle; chill.

Notes
• See also my suggestions for using Dark Chocolate Mousse as the basis for other desserts; the White Chocolate Mousse will work well with all of them, and I use it more often as a basis for other desserts than on its own.

Instant Microwave Sponge Pudding

SERVES 4

50g unsalted butter
50g caster sugar
1 egg, beaten
75g plain flour, sifted
half teaspoon baking powder

To serve:
120ml Butterscotch Sauce (page 121)

1 Cream the butter and sugar together.
2 Add the egg, flour and baking powder.
3 Put the mixture into four greased ramekins; they should be half full. Microwave one pudding for 1 minute on full power.

4 Check that the pudding is cooked, by inserting a fine skewer, which should come out clean. If not, microwave for 20 seconds more; thereafter, check at 10 second intervals.
5 Repeat the process with the other three puddings and then microwave all four puddings together for 1 minute on a medium power.
6 Turn out and serve with warm Butterscotch Sauce.

Notes
• If not using as a quick base for Cambridge Pudding (page 158), serve with chocolate sauce or toffee sauce; or add the juice and zest of two lemons to the mixture above, for a lemon sponge. Many variations work.

Cambridge Pudding

This is one of our most popular desserts at the Pink Geranium later on in the year. We have to have this on the menu, of course, because we're so near Cambridge. It's a classic pudding and the recipe really does seem to have originated from Cambridge. We've adapted the recipe a little, by adding a few spices.

It does take a while to steam, but the recipe can be adapted to allow it to be cooked in the microwave. It is very much a winter pudding and we serve it with butterscotch sauce or ice cream melting over the top (see photo).

SERVES 6

180g suet
180g plain flour
180g cake crumbs
1 teaspoon baking powder
180g mixed dried fruit
120g granulated sugar
1 teaspoon ground mixed spice
300ml milk

To serve:
Butterscotch Sauce (page 121) or vanilla ice cream

1 Mix all the dry ingredients together.
2 Add the milk and mix well.
3 Put in greased individual moulds, allowing for the mixture to rise by up to 25 per cent. Cover with pleated foil and tie round with string. Put the puddings on a trivet in a large pan or steamer, pour in water.
4 Steam for 45 minutes.
5 Turn out and serve with the sauce or ice cream.

 A Sauternes.

Notes
• I like to marinate the mixed dried fruit in a little brandy (enough to cover) for about an hour beforehand.
• If cooking by microwave, use these ingredients, but halve the milk and add 100g soft butter. Follow the same stages as Instant Microwave Pudding (page 157), adding the various spices, crumbs and suet at stage 2. Bake for 1½-2 minutes on the high setting.

Lime Tart
with *Crème Chantilly*

Here's a bet. If you follow this recipe carefully I will wager that it's the best lime tart you've ever had. Tell me if it's not. Or use lemon, and I will bet it's the best lemon tart you've ever had too.

We've perfected this tart over a number of years; the secret is to cook it in a low oven so that it doesn't rise or soufflé. The other secret is to take the tart out when it still seems not quite cooked ... the wobble factor must be there! It will then set as it cools.

The tart is very sharp tasting and needs something sweet, like *Crème Chantilly*, or ice cream, with it. When it's cut into wedges, you could dredge it in icing sugar and blow-torch the top, to caramelize it. If you haven't got a blow torch, try using a hot grill, covering the pastry to stop it burning. This gives it a sort of *crème brûlée* topping, which is very appetizing and attractive too.

MAKES A 25CM TART

25cm sweet pastry case, baked blind (page 149)

For the filling:
grated zest and juice of 10 limes
250ml double cream
5 whole eggs
100g caster sugar

To serve:
***Crème Chantilly* (page 119)**

1 Preheat the oven to 150°C/300°F/Gas Mark 2. Mix all the filling ingredients together and pour them into the pastry case.
2 Bake for about 40 minutes. The filling should not rise at all at this low temperature and you should remove the tart while the centre is still slightly wobbly. Leave to cool.
3 Cut into neat wedges and serve with *Crème Chantilly*.

 Late-harvest Australian Riesling.

Notes
• Allow the tart to cool completely before cutting it.

Classic (but brilliant) *Crème Brûlée*

I've never used anything other than this recipe and it's always worked brilliantly. Use fresh vanilla pods; the seeds in the egg yolks and the vanilla pods in the cream.

The secret is the use of the *bain marie*. Cover it with foil, which must be pierced. Once I did not pierce it, and the foil created a vacuum; the *crème brûlées* souffléd and over-cooked. Another idea is to warm the water a little first, to speed up the cooking process.

The wobble factor comes in here too (see Lime Tart). When the portions are totally cold, cover with icing sugar, not caster sugar, and use a blow torch evenly to glaze the surface.

SERVES 4

1 vanilla pod
5 egg yolks
600ml double cream
75-100g icing sugar, to taste

1 Preheat the oven to 125°C/275°F/Gas Mark 2. Cut the vanilla pod in half and remove the seeds. Put the seeds into the egg yolks and the pod into the cream.
2 Bring the cream slowly to the boil and gradually whisk it into the egg yolks; remove the pod and add sugar to taste.
3 Pour the mixture into four large ramekins and bake in a *bain marie*, covered with pierced foil, and bake in the oven for

45 minutes, or until nearly set. The middle of the filling should still be wobbly.
4 Once cooked, remove from the *bain marie* and allow to cool and set.
5 When completely cold, cover the top of the *brûlées* with more icing sugar and either grill them or use a blow torch, to glaze the top carefully. Serve immediately.

 A good Sauternes.

Notes
• You can flavour the *crème brûlée* with additions like jasmine, by adding it to the cream. (Simply soak a jasmine tea bag in the warm mixture to create an infusion – don't add any more liquid.) You'll need to taste the cream to be sure it's strong enough, and after adding the flavour, pass the mixture through a sieve before it goes into ramekins. *Crème brûlée* ice cream is delicious if you add this mix to your ice cream maker (or sorbetière). Make chocolate crème brûlée by melting chocolate and adding to the cream and eggs. Add as much as you like; the more you use, the richer the chocolate taste and the quicker it will cook so keep an eye on it (it may only take half the time). You can also flavour *crème brûlée* with liqueurs or finely grated orange zest and juice.
• One nice touch is to add liqueur and then serve a glass of it with the *crème brûlée* Your guests can alternately sip their drinks and eat the *brûlée*.

Rich Chocolate Marquise
with mocha sauce

Another great dinner party pudding. People love chocolate and this is easy to do. In the photograph, I've put spun sugar on the top for a more spectacular effect.

The sponge in this recipe is arranged around the marquise which keeps the terrine a nice neat shape when it's cut, but you don't have to use it either – I didn't for the photo!

SERVES 8

1 Tree Cake (page 148) (optional)

For the marquise:
300g dark chocolate
170g honey
100g unsalted butter, softened
250ml double cream
4 egg yolks
75ml coffee liqueur or Tia Maria

To serve:
mocha sauce (*Crème Anglaise*, page 120, flavoured with chocolate and coffee)

1 If using to line the marquise, make and bake the sponge. Turn the sponge out to rest on a cooling rack and then cut it into thin slices and soak in a little liqueur or brandy.

To make the marquise:
1 Melt the chocolate and honey together over a bowl of hot, not boiling, water. It's important that the water doesn't touch the bowl.
2 Cream the butter and partially whip the double cream.
3 Add the cream and butter to the chocolate mixture. Add the egg yolks and liqueur and mix them in well.

4 Line a large terrine mould with cling film and then with strips of thin sponge, if using this. Cover the bottom and sides of the mould completely.
5 Pour the marquise mixture into the mould; chill to set.
6 To serve, carefully warm the mould in a bowl of boiling water (or use your blow torch) and turn out the marquise. Cut into 1cm slices and, ideally, serve with a little mocha sauce, or blackcurrant coulis.

WINE Californian Essencia Orange Muscat.

Notes
• A bowl of water, which will turn to steam in the oven during cooking, makes the sponge slightly lighter.
• Spun sugar is very easy to do, even though it sounds complicated, but make sure you cover the floor as it's also messy. Make it with 4 parts sugar to 1 water, brought to a caramel (160°C) in a pan over a low heat. Make sure the environment is cool but not cold, and that the sugar mixture has started to cool a little before you start to spin it or it will just fall straight down on to the floor. Take a spun sugar whisk (like a normal whisk, but with the filaments forming prongs rather than loops), spoon or fork and then just throw the mixture over a clean broom handle or chopsticks, stringing it out by passing each whiskful back and forth over the stick, and creating a thick candy-floss effect. Gather it up and put it on to the terrine. Repeat for each serving, or split a large ball up into portions – it should divide quite easily, be formed a little in your hands, and should hold its shape for up to an hour.
• Chocolate marquise also works very well with blackcurrant coulis or various fruit; the photograph shows it garnished with blueberries. See also my suggestion for a marquise Swiss roll (page 148) using Tree Cake.

Steven's Bread and Butter Pudding
including bread and butter pudding soufflé

This is a very good, very classic bread and butter pudding recipe – the best you'll ever find.

The secret here is that we make an Anglaise Sauce, instead of just using milk and eggs and we use home-made brioche, if possible. Also, and this is a case of in-for-a-penny-in-for-a-pound, we soak the raisins and fruit in brandy before using them. These three things make an amazing difference to the finished product.

You can adapt the recipe by adding the zest of the oranges or orange juice, to take the sweetness of the dish off slightly, but it's really nice as it is. After cooking, you could also dust it with icing sugar and then use a blow torch or grill carefully to caramelize the top (see photo on page 151).

125g sultanas
125g raisins
120ml cooking brandy
225g unsalted butter
10-12 brioche or white bread slices
225g soft brown sugar
475ml *Crème Anglaise* (page 120)
grated zest and juice of 2 oranges (optional)

1 Marinate the sultanas and raisins in the brandy for about an hour. Preheat the oven to 190°C/375°F/Gas Mark 5.
2 Butter the brioche or bread slices on both sides. Cut them into triangles and arrange them in a buttered baking dish.
3 Cover this layer with the marinated sultanas and raisins and any unabsorbed brandy. Sprinkle liberally with the soft brown sugar. Cover this layer with *Crème Anglaise*.
4 Repeat this procedure until your baking dish is overfilled (you won't need all the *Crème Anglaise*).
5 Cover with foil and bake for about 30 minutes. Remove the foil and cook the pudding for a further 15 minutes, to crispen the top.

6 Serve by cutting into neat rounds with a straight-sided metal pastry cutter (see photos), dust with icing sugar and serve with the remaining *Crème Anglaise*. It will cut cleaner and better when cold.

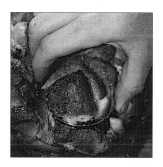

A good Sauternes, or Château Climens.

For Bread and Butter Soufflé:

• When you cut the pudding out in rounds, you end up with lots of little bits left over. Put these in the food processor and blend them to a smooth paste. Add a tiny bit of sweet soufflé base (page 94) and whisked egg whites, and blend everything together. Put this into buttered and sugared ramekins and then you have a wonderful bread and butter pudding soufflé, which works brilliantly with Butterscotch Sauce poured into the middle of it. Two recipes for the price of one.

Note

The addition of fruit, like blueberries, raspberries or strawberries is a nice addition to each layer as you build. As always, experiment a little!

Ice Creams

Whatever anybody says, I believe you need an ice cream maker to make perfect ice cream. We have tried to make ice cream by hand at the restaurant but the results are poor in comparison. There are some inexpensive domestic versions available which both freeze and mix the ice cream. Follow the instructions relevant to your particular model of machine; these recipes are all for the custard which you place in the machine, then let it do the work!

The simplest and most effective way of producing ice cream is to make *Crème Anglaise*, page 120. The great thing is that you can make wonderful flavours that you won't see in the shops. The basil variation, for example, may seem bizarre, but does work brilliantly. If you do buy a machine, experiment with flavours.

For white chocolate ice cream:
6 egg yolks
250ml milk
250ml double cream
seeds of 1 vanilla pod
150g white chocolate, melted

Prepare as the Anglaise Sauce and add the melted chocolate at the last stage, just before the final pass through a sieve before it enters the machine.

Brown bread ice cream
Lightly toast five slices of brown bread and make them into crumbs. Add to the *Anglaise* instead of the melted chocolate.

Maple syrup ice cream
Add about 125g maple syrup to the *Anglaise*, instead of the melted chocolate.

Basil ice cream
Infuse a large bunch of basil, chopped, in the *Anglaise* whilst warm, for 30 minutes. Pass through a sieve and add the leaves of a small bunch of basil, finely *chiffonaded* (shredded), before finally putting the mixture in the machine.

Crème brûlee ice cream
Simply follow the recipe for *Crème Brûlee* (page 161), and use as an ice cream mixture. Serve with icing sugar glazed with your blow torch, if you have one, and serve immediately.

Notes
• If you don't have an ice cream machine, you can par-freeze these mixtures, whisk, and freeze again. Repeat this at least three times, until you reach your desired consistency.

Garnishes and Other Accompaniments

Good food should never be garnished with anything alien to the dish. For example, a sprig of tarragon is unwelcome on a dish that doesn't involve tarragon; however, a sprig of chervil is fine, as it has a much milder flavour and will not change the flavours of the dish. Salad garnishes used in this book are used to add texture, flavour and colour to first courses. The leaves should always be dressed and seasoned; thus they come to play an important part in the dish. Most main dishes need little or no garnish; the addition of well cooked vegetables (see the photographs for ideas) and a colourful sauce is enough. Some dishes may require a garnish of deep fried herbs or a sprig of chervil – but that's all please!

Classy food is food that looks very simple on the plate, yet at the same time appear extremely colourful. I believe it's better to have no garnish on a dish than one that's tired or wilting or irrelevant.The days of tomato roses and Chinese cut radishes are best forgotten. However, food is like fashion: what goes round, comes round. So watch this space!

Herb Crust

A herb crust is particularly good on fish baked in the oven or fried; all the flavours of the garlic and herbs cook into the fish. I particularly like this recipe for spicing up a piece of salmon and another good use is for coating goat's cheese before frying it.

170g fresh, preferably white, breadcrumbs
60g fresh parsley
30g fresh basil
30g fresh coriander

1 garlic clove
30g unsalted butter, softened (or 3-4 tablespoons olive oil)
salt and pepper

1 Put all the ingredients, except the butter, in a food processor and mix until thoroughly blended, so that it becomes a pleasant green colour.
2 Add the butter and blend it in.
3 Mould the mixture thinly as a crust on top of your fish and bake or fry as required.

Herb Breadcrumbs

You can use many different types of bread; brioche is especially good. Use any herbs that you fancy, as well. If you want a darker, crisper crumb, dry the bread in the oven first, until it's crisp and brown.

half a loaf of bread, preferably home-made
large bunch of fresh coriander or herb of your choice
salt and pepper

Tear the bread into small pieces. Put it into the food processor and add the herbs. Blend until you have fine crumbs. Season.

Deep-fried Vegetables

In a similar way to herbs, vegetables can benefit from deep-frying. I have chosen leeks as an example (I strongly recommend these) but you can try a range of vegetables. Celeriac, salsify, carrots, celery, courgettes and aubergine all work brilliantly.

1 leek
plain flour
about 200ml cooking oil
salt

1 *Chiffonade* (finely shred) a leek into small julienne (matchstick) strips, avoiding the green, dirty part of the leek. Toss them in seasoned flour and shake off the excess.
2 Heat about 200ml of cooking oil in a saucepan to approximately 170°C. Test the temperature by dipping one leek strip into the oil. The oil should bubble but the leek should not brown too quickly.
3 Deep-fry the remaining leeks until slightly brown – about 30 seconds – and then drain them on kitchen paper, to remove excess oil.
4 Season with salt and arrange in a tower shape.

Deep-fried Herbs

This is a trendy way to serve herbs. The style adds colour, texture and crispness to a dish. You can also deep-fry celery leaves, or other, larger leaves, such as spinach.

about 200ml cooking oil
herbs of your choice
salt

Heat the oil to about 170°C. Drop the herbs into the oil at arm's length (beware of the of the oil spitting due to the water in the herbs). Remove with a perforated spoon after 6-10 seconds. Drain on kitchen paper. Season with salt and serve scattered around the dish.

Confit of Garlic

This is a good way of cooking garlic to remove its strength and bitterness and add a sweetness to it. It works well with lamb, chicken, beef and most game.

You will need both foil and baking parchment (or greaseproof paper) for this recipe.

12 garlic cloves
15ml sweet wine
fresh thyme sprig
60g unsalted butter
pinch of freshly grated nutmeg
1 piece of star anise (optional)
1 dessertspoon olive oil
salt and pepper

1 Preheat the oven to 230°C/450°F/Gas Mark 8. Put the garlic cloves in the centre of a large circle of foil, with a similarly sized circle of baking parchment underneath (**a**).
2 Pour over the wine and add all the other ingredients.
3 Fold the circle over and make a pouch (**b**). Bake on a baking tray until the pouch rises and the parchment browns (**c**, about 20 minutes).
4 Carefully open the pouch (**d**), remove the garlic cloves and serve immediately.

Notes
• The addition of the olive oil prevents the butter from burning and over-colouring the garlic cloves. Garlic cooked in this way becomes sweet and tender, and can therefore be eaten in whole clove form to accompany a dish.
• You can also blend the *confit* in the food processor, with added flour, to make a thick paste and then form it into quenelles (a small egg-shaped scoop, made with a spoon; see photos **e** to **h**). Deep-fry the quenelles to make good *beignets* (see page 13).

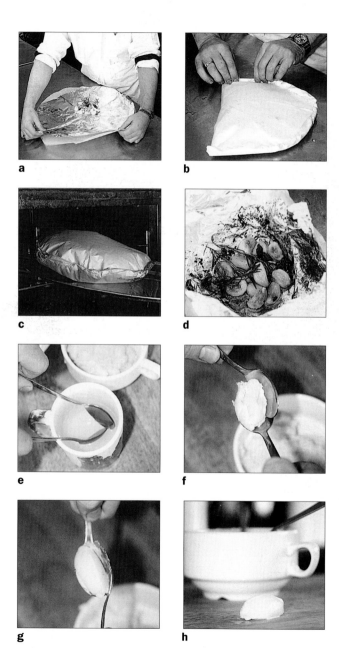

a

b

c

d

e

f

g

h

Pasta

We all seem to know or have a home-made pasta recipe, although many people I have met feel that the process makes too much mess and the results aren't really worth the effort. OK, pasta does make a bit of a mess, but it certainly is worth it: easy to prepare and delicious to eat.

Firstly, forget any previous recipes. This is the one! Secondly, although you can take a long time over the preparation, remember that I did this recipe on *Ready Steady Cook* in 20 minutes, cooked and served with a tomato fondue and pan-seared mushrooms and the works ... so it can't be that much trouble.

You do need a good strong flour for the very best results. The best kinds are Italian strong white bread flour, usually labelled '00', of which several brands are available; try Italian delicatessens. Ordinary strong flour will do instead. Strong flour has more gluten, which makes the dough more elastic, so you can have a lower proportion of flour to the other ingredients and still have a manageable dough.

MAKES ABOUT 1KG (ENOUGH FOR ABOUT 10-12 PEOPLE)

3 whole eggs
5 egg yolks
pinch of salt
1 teaspoon olive oil, preferably virgin or extra virgin
about 450g strong Italian pasta flour

1 Crack the whole eggs and yolks into a food processor (or an electric mixer with a dough hook) and add the salt (**a**).
2 Blend until smooth (**b**) and add a dash of olive oil.
3 Add the flour, spoon by spoon, with the food processor running, until the mixture forms a dry dough (**c**). Knead it a little (**d**); it shouldn't be sticky, though.
4 Ideally, the mixture should be rolled into a ball wrapped in cling film (**e** and **f**)and refrigerated to rest it (about an hour for

best results). Alternatively, if you are short of time you must add a little more flour to the dough.
5 Pass the dough through your pasta machine from number 1 to number 6, so that it is rolled into a long, thin strip (**g**). Now pass it through the cutting section of the machine, to form linguini or tagliatelle (**h**), or roll (**i**), and cut, without passing it through the machine (see Notes), into 12cm squares, to create ravioli (see page 135).
6 To cook the pasta, simply blanch it in boiling, salted water with a little olive oil. When the water comes back to the boil, remove the pasta and immediately refresh it in iced water. When it's completely cold, place it on a tray and pour over a little oil, to stop it from sticking to itself.
7 When you need to serve the pasta, warm it gently in a saucepan, with butter and plenty of seasoning and add a chopped, soft green herb of your choice.

Notes
• Rolling pasta by hand is no easy matter and you cannot really produce as fine a result by hand as you can using a pasta machine. Since so many simple dishes can be made from fresh pasta, a pasta machine (which is not expensive) is a good investment. Fix the machine on to the side of a table and flour it well before use. Cut the dough into quarters, flattened slightly with the rolling pin. Roll the dough using the thickest setting and repeat, thinning it each time on a finer setting, until the pasta is about 2.5mm thick (setting 6 or 7).
• Depending on the strength of the flour, you will need more or less water. When rolling out the dough, use no flour, or as little as possible; if too much is absorbed, the pasta will become glutinous and slimy when cooked. I use cling film to wrap the pasta while it's resting, to prevent a crust from forming.
• If you are not using the pasta immediately, drape it loosely

(continued)

a

b

c

d

e

f

g

h

i

on a tray to dry. Dried pasta can be stored in an airtight container for three to four weeks. For freezing, place the freshly cut pasta in a large container and seal it. It will keep for up to three weeks.

To flavour or colour the dough (see photo page 167):
• *Tomato pasta:* simply add 1 dessertspoon tomato purée to the eggs before processing them.
• *Spinach pasta:* boil a large handful of spinach until it has absorbed most of the water. Squeeze out and purée in your food processor. Add to the eggs before processing them.

• *Coriander pasta:* this is the same as spinach but use half spinach, half coriander leaves (the spinach helps the colour).
• *Basil pasta:* the same as above.
• *Black pasta:* follow the recipe and add 2 sachets of squid ink to the eggs after processing them.
• To make a pasta tower, which is used as a garnish in several recipes, use a meat fork to scoop up a serving (about 50g) linguine-shaped pasta. Hold the fork in one hand and twist it with the other, to create a high, circular whirl of pasta. Lift and twist the fork to extricate it from the pasta, leaving a tower of pasta (see photos **a** to **f**).

a

b

c

d

e

f

make many references to cooking vegetables to serve as garnishes and accompaniments throughout these recipes. Here is a list of my favourites and my preferred methods.

ENGLISH SPINACH

The best way to cook this is to remove the stalks and wash the leaves thoroughly. Blanch them in boiling water for a minute. Remove the leaves with a slotted or draining spoon and put them straight into ice-cold water (preferably with ice) to refresh them. Gently squeeze the leaves, to extract excess water, and, when you need the spinach hot, pan-fry it in a little butter and oil, with salt, freshly grated nutmeg and freshly ground white pepper. Drain and serve immediately. Young spinach leaves can be simply fried without blanching.

A bed of spinach can be served under both fish and meat and goes very well with a range of vegetarian recipes.

Young spinach is best fried straight away without blanching.

CABBAGE

Cabbage is generally classed according to both the season (spring, summer, etc.) and the type (semi-hearted, green, hard white, red, etc.). Spring cabbages are loose-leaved and small-hearted, Savoy cabbage (my favourite) is green-hearted, spring greens are young cabbages with no hearts.

Young cabbage is best *chiffonaded* (finely shredded) and fried in butter and/or oil, with freshly grated nutmeg and seasoning. Older (late-season) cabbage is best blanched first, then drained and finished in a pan, with a little double cream, seasoning, nutmeg and perhaps a little caraway.

GLAZED CARROTS

Carrots can be made interesting by peeling them with a potato peeler to achieve an even thickness throughout. Then place them in cold water with chopped fresh coriander, seasoning, unsalted butter and honey. Quantities vary depending on amounts but, generally, the same rule applies as for Baby Carrots (page 177). Once the pan is boiling and the carrots are tender, remove and refresh them under cold running water. Now slice through the carrot thinly at an angle, to create lozenge shapes and finish by frying them in a hot pan, with a little unsalted butter and oil, salt and sugar to glaze them. Serve scattered around the dish.

FRENCH BEANS

Prepare French beans by topping and tailing them, being careful not to remove too much of the bean, and plunging them into vigorously boiling water that contains salt and a little unsalted butter. Cook the beans for 2 minutes, before draining and refreshing them under cold running water. To re-heat, simply blanch them again for a minute, drain them and toss them in a little melted unsalted butter and salt, with a hint of freshly ground white pepper.

MANGE-TOUT AND SUGAR-SNAP PEAS

Prepare mange-tout peas by picking the tops and tails off and cooking as for French beans, but for 1 minute only. Drain and serve immediately. Sugar-snap peas need a little longer, say 2-3 minutes, but both should be cooked and served immediately and not blanched, refreshed and then re-heated. Season with a little unsalted butter, salt and ground white pepper.

CELERIAC

This knobbly root vegetable has the most delectable aroma when peeled and chopped. Peel it with a very sharp knife and chop it into small cubes; barely cover with water, add a knob of unsalted butter, season and boil until tender. When soft, drain and mash with a potato masher. Add a little more unsalted butter and cream and check the seasoning. Finish with freshly grated nutmeg and freshly ground white pepper. A good soup can also be made from the celeriac purée.

GLOBE ARTICHOKES

To prepare globe artichokes, cut away at the leaves to reveal the heart (photos **a** to **e**). Immediately immerse the hearts in the juice of at least four lemons and then place in a bowl of water containing the juice of a further two or three lemons (**f**). If you wish, slice the hearts between the two immersions (**g** and **h**). This will help keep them white; if they turn grey they can become almost inedible when cooked!

To cook them, follow the instructions for making a *Blanc* (page 136) and ensure you tip the juice of the four lemons into the blanc, with a little olive oil and plenty of seasoning. Add the artichokes, bring to the boil gently and, when the knife slides into the artichoke easily (this usually takes 20-30 minutes cooking), remove the saucepan from the heat and allow the artichokes to cool in the *blanc*.

When cold, carefully remove the choke from the centre of each heart with a small teaspoon. An artichoke purée can be made by processing the hearts with a little double cream and further seasoning.

Once cooked and cooled, artichokes can be marinated in olive oil with garlic, herbs, shallots and a little balsamic vinegar and then taken straight from the marinade on to your char-griddle. Alternatively, sear them in a very hot frying-pan. You can vary the flavours of your marinade, according to your own tastes. Cooked in a *blanc* and then marinated, the flavours are unbelievable.

PARSNIPS

Peel your parsnips and cut them into small batons. Marinate them for about 30 minutes in olive oil, with thyme, lemon juice and honey (mix this together first). Season the parsnips and then roast them on a roasting tray in a hot oven (230°C/450°F/Gas Mark 8) until crispy and tender. These also make the basis for a good soup when puréed.

An excellent purée can be made by cutting the parsnips a little larger in the first instance and roasting in the same way until tender but not crisp or too coloured. Mash or process

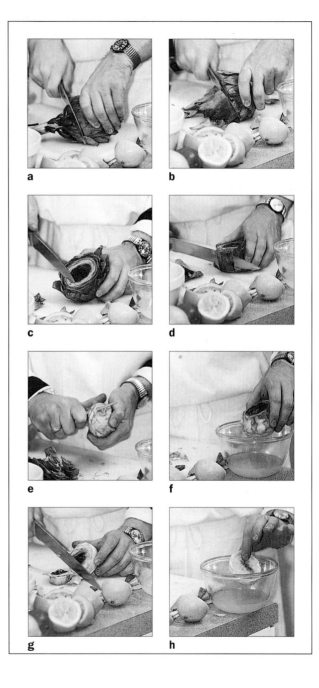

a b

c d

e f

g h

the parsnips to a purée and season well. Finish with a little olive oil to bind it together in a heavy saucepan and, ideally, serve with meat.

Brilliant soup can be made by using the same purée and then adding double cream, a little nutmeg and a little dry white wine. It is very rich but makes an excellent winter warming soup, which I use at the Pink Geranium every year.

ASPARAGUS/SAMPHIRE

These two are not really connected but samphire often gets called sea asparagus because it looks similar. Samphire grows in the marshes on the river/sea banks and hence tastes rather salty and almost fishy. It is excellent blanched as for French beans and then fried in unsalted butter, with plenty of lemon juice and nutmeg. Serve with fish, preferably underneath the fish.

Asparagus comes in all sizes and from all over Europe, the Middle East and Far East. There are about 20 varieties but the most common is green asparagus (the thinner stalks are known as sprues). In my opinion, English asparagus is the best, but this has only a short season.

People often (always!) squabble over how best to cook asparagus: to steam it, boil it, heads out of the water, in the water, tied, etc., etc. My feeling is treat it like other light green vegetables, such as French beans. Trim to size first; we cut it into about 8cm lengths (using the cut-off stalks for asparagus soup). Plunge into well seasoned, boiling water and cook for about 3 minutes. When tender, remove and refresh under cold running water or serve immediately, tossed in a little melted unsalted butter, salt and white pepper and a squeeze of lemon juice. Baby asparagus is excellent with fish dishes and complements other baby vegetables well, both in colour and flavour.

Baby Vegetables

Spring brings the first budding English baby vegetables, with the arrival of a little warmth and sunshine. I am always delighted to be able to use the first baby carrots, turnips and leeks, as they make a dish look colourful and sophisticated and at the same time add dimension, texture and great flavours to food. You can see this in the photographs throughout this book.

In the winter, baby vegetables can be expensive and, like other intensively farmed or forced products, they quite often taste of very little, being both watery and bland. I recommend avoiding out-of-season baby vegetables. Like other vegetables, baby vegetables have a 'special' way that they should be treated and cooked. Below are some of my favourites and how you can best handle them.

BRAISED BABY AUBERGINES

Because aubergines have quite leathery skins and, in baby form, a watery flesh, they are best gently braised.

about 12 baby aubergines, halved lengthways
bunch of fresh coriander
400ml orange juice (or juice of 6 fresh oranges)
1 teaspoon freshly grated nutmeg
2 tablespoons fresh olive oil
salt and pepper

Preheat the oven to 220°C/425°F/Gas Mark 7. Put the aubergines in a baking dish, cover with other ingredients. Cover dish with foil and bake for about 30 minutes, or until tender. Allow to rest, then serve as a garnish alongside the other vegetables. They reheat well once braised.

BABY CARROTS

To prepare these, use a small paring knife (**a**) or potato peeler (**b**) and scrape gently from the green stalks to the root. Ensure that you peel around the top of the stalk trying not to remove the stalks, which are attractive for presentation. Leave 2-3cm stalks on the carrots (**c**). The point of peeling around the stalk is to remove any dirt trapped there.

To cook the baby carrots, simply put them in a pan, covered with cold water, add salt, a large knob of unsalted butter and about 2 dessert-spoons of caster sugar (or one large dessertspoon of honey) per 16-18 carrots. A sprig of coriander or tarragon also adds to the flavour.

Bring the water to the boil and, when your knife slides easily into the carrots, drain and refresh them under cold running water. Reserve until you need to re-heat them.

a

b

c

BABY TURNIPS

These can be prepared in the same way as baby carrots, by scraping and cleaning. Try not to remove too much of the turnip. Cook them in a *Blanc* (page 136), to ensure they stay white, then refresh under cold running water and reserve them as for carrots.

BABY LEEKS

These tiny versions are so much like spring onions to look at and taste you can hardly tell the difference! They aren't so gritty as full-grown leeks, so need less cleaning. Just discard the very green tops (which, like spring onion tops, can be finely chopped and used as a herb garnish). Cook them very briefly in boiling, seasoned water, with a knob of unsalted butter, until just tender; remove and refresh under cold running water.

Salad Leaves

You should look for some of the more adventurous leaves, if you really want to impress and experiment. Try, for example, exotic varieties such as rocket, lamb's lettuce or dandelion. More readily available will be oak leaf, lollo rosso, curly frisée (endive) and radicchio. Always mix more than one type of leaf in salads.

The way that you use the leaves is important to the finish of the dish. Leaves should always be dressed, seasoned and neatly arranged. They can be prepared in advance and chilled if your fridge is big enough, the plates stacked on top of each other with the metal rings still in place, keeping them apart. These are the two principal salads that I recommend.

CIRCLE SALAD (a)

This salad garnish is widely used throughout this book, to dress around a dish. The main ingredients sit in the middle of the plate, at the centre of attention, dressed and garnished only by little florets of colourful leaves, which add another dimension to the dish. The Goat's Cheese Tapenade is an excellent example of how well this works, for the cheese would be a little lonesome without the company of leaves. Simply place a circular object or pastry cutter in the centre of the dish, and arrange a selection of leaves around it.

CENTRE SALAD (b)

To give a dish some height and colour (imagine three scallops alone on a plate) a centre salad is frequently needed. Again, it adds flavours and textures to dish, but most importantly it gives a sense of presentation to whatever is circled around it. In the reverse method to the above, layer leaves inside a plain metal ring; remove ring gently before arranging food.

Roasted Vegetables

A brilliant way to give a dish a rustic image, these are delicious and easily prepared. You can use a wide variety of vegetables, especially other root vegetables.

carrots, leeks, and celery (or other vegetables), prepared
2 tablespoons caster sugar
oil, for frying
salt and pepper

1 Cut the carrots into thickish strips. Fry these, about three per person, on top of the stove in an ovenproof pan in a little oil, with salt and a pinch of sugar, and then add the cut leek, followed, after a few minutes, by the cut celery. Caramelize the vegetables in the pan, giving them colour.

2 Place your ovenproof pan in the hot oven for about 15 minutes, or until vegetables are quite tender.

Mediterranean Vegetables

I often describe dishes as being accompanied by Mediterranean vegetables. By this I mean vegetables that are indigenous to the Mediterranean region.

PEPPERS

Roasted peppers are easy to prepare and very delicious (see page 62). Once roasted, peeled (after roasting) and cooled they can be marinated in olive oil with garlic and rosemary for brilliant flavours. To re-heat, simply pan-fry or roast until hot.

AUBERGINES

These taste best fried in a hot pan, with a little olive oil, or cooked on the griddle pan. This gives them crispness on the outside, with softness in the centre. They don't need to be marinated; just season with salt and white pepper before frying. Don't use too much oil as this will make them greasy. (See photo on page 86.)

COURGETTES

Courgettes come in many shapes and sizes and two colours, yellow and green. They both taste the same, and can be quite bitter. To bring out the Mediterranean flavours of this vegetable – which, at its best, is superb – cut thinly into elongated lozenges, marinate in olive oil with garlic and rosemary or thyme and then char-griddle them for both flavour and a wonderfully attractive marking (see photo on page 86). Courgettes are ideal for garnishing rustic, chunky Mediterranean fish, such as monkfish, lobster, red mullet and sea bass.

TOMATOES

A fruit or a vegetable? Either way, tomatoes are wonderful roasted and served with green and other Mediterranean-style vegetables. To roast, simply heat an ovenproof frying-pan until red hot and, in the tiniest drop of oil, fry until coloured (2-5 minutes); then roast in a hot oven for 5 minutes until soft but not mushy. Season well and serve. They make a great pairing with caramelized onions and marinate well after they have been roasted in garlic and herb oils.

FENNEL

Very pungent so be careful where and how you use it. Great with fish, it is best braised in a light vegetable stock, with white wine, unsalted butter, salt and pepper and a fresh soft green herb (coriander and tarragon). Once it is soft enough that your knife slides into it, remove from the braising stock and serve.

Index to Recipes